THE GREAT
ECONOMIC
DECEPTION

HOW ECONOMICS ARE BEING
WEAPONIZED AGAINST OUR FREEDOMS

THERESA YAROSH

FREILING
PUBLISHING

Published by Freiling Publishing,
a division of Freiling Agency, LLC.
P.O. Box 1264
Warrenton, VA 20188

www.FreilingPublishing.com

Paperback ISBN: 978-1-956267-38-9
eBook ISBN: 978-1-956267-39-6

Printed in the United States of America

All the Glory belongs
to the Lord Jesus Christ
I am
Created for a Purpose
Rooted In Christ

"Therefore, as you received Christ Jesus the Lord, so walk in him,
rooted and built up in him and established in the faith,
just as you were taught, abounding in thanksgiving."

Colossians 2:6-7

September 2022

Dear Kathy,

I hope you enjoy reading this book as much as I enjoyed writing it. I sit on the board of the Center for Garden State Families and have written many of the articles that go out via email.

Continue to pray for the nation and the state of New Jersey.

May God Bless You!

Colossians 2:8

ENDORSEMENTS

"Worldview matters! How you form your view of the world around you determines how you live, love, and treat others. Theresa Yarosh lays out the condition of our society and links it to pivotal events in history. History does repeat itself and those of us who have learned from history are determined not to fall into the despotism of ages past. Theresa exposes our current state of events. She brings to light how past mistakes are happening all over again. *The Great Economic Deception* is a warning and a call to return to our foundations. The time to wake up is now. For if we don't we are doomed to lose our individuality and every freedom we enjoy."

–Rev. Gregory Quinlan, President and Founder,
The Center for Garden State Families

"Theresa Yarosh has clearly laid out why our US economy and culture are suffering from a catastrophic collapsing condition. She has masterfully highlighted key movements and complex characters in this precise, meticulously researched, and beautifully written volume. Through Theresa's brilliant prose the reader learns much personal information about influential personalities and one by one the puzzle pieces fit together. In addition, Theresa has viewed this process from a biblical point of view and any reader can be enlightened as to why our once powerful nation is now facing such peril. This gem of a book can well serve as a guide to anyone who seeks to learn from the past to improve the future and those interested in observing God's hand in our history will be doubly blessed."

–Gabriella Brandeal, MA, Director of Education
from The Center for Garden State Families

CONTENTS

ACKNOWLEDGMENTS

*"Two are better than one, because they
have a good reward for their labor."*
Ecclesiastes 4:9

THIS BOOK HAS resulted from over a year and a half of writing. First and foremost, it is dedicated to my Lord and Savior, Jesus Christ. Through the Holy Spirit, He is the one who has directed my labors and my words. I am grateful for His direction in bringing this book to completion. Many are acknowledged for their encouragement, support, and friendship. I want to begin by thanking Tom Freiling and the entire staff of Freiling Publishing. Tom, it has always been my dream to write a book. I feel that our being put in touch with one another has been very providential and for a time such as this. I want to thank Reverend Gregory Quinlan and Gabriella "Gay" Brandeal of The Center For Garden State Families. Greg and Gay, if it were not for your willingness to allow me to write for our blog, this book would never have come to fruition. Greg, you were right all along; I was writing my book and needed a supportive platform to begin the process. Gay, I want to thank you for being there as my editor and reviewing everything I have written. You will always be my dear friend and "editorial director" in life.

Through the years, I have been blessed to have many friends who have come into my life, each bringing their unique gifts that would change and influence my own life for the better. In many ways, the things we do are not an individual effort but the melding together of all the relationships that God puts into our lives so that, in the end, the very best of who we are is revealed. In this regard, I cannot help but think of my dear friend

Mary Tortorello who did just that—bring out the best in me. Mary, you were the one who inspired my second company Main Street Medigap, and for that, I will always be grateful. Our friendship motivated me to continue my studies and pursue the Certified Kingdom Advisor® Designation. Your loving kindness and encouragement are like treasured gifts to me. I also want to thank Liesja Tortorello. Liesja, because of my friendship with your mom, I have seized the day, and the words of your essay Carpe Diem will never be forgotten (John 16:22).

As I write the acknowledgment pages of this book, I am enjoying time with my sisters in the Lord Catherine Kelly and Mary Ann Geary in the Finger Lakes in New York. I greatly appreciate these times we have together as we spend time in the Word of God to reflect and renew our hearts in Christ. I also want to thank Steven Geary for reading my work and the book-light gift. Now I can not only read more, but I can also write more books. I also want to thank my friend Julie Merrill for being my career development supervisor at the Guardian, always having confidence in me, and lifting me up in all my endeavors. I want to thank Carlin and Joe Meditz for being there for me as friends and for all the great weekends I have spent with you. I also want to thank Josh, Clarissa, and Caleb Kostenko. Thank you for making me feel like a part of your family. It has meant a lot to me over the years. I want to thank Mindy Geary for our long-standing friendship and all the insight and wisdom you have given me over the years. I want to thank Debbie and Richie Ingenito for their friendship. Debbie, I think a breakfast celebration is now in order. I also want to thank Mark Kapsky for being a part of my second company Main Street Medigap and always giving me the support I need to continue growing and expanding my business. Mark, I could not think of a better person to be part of my company. You are a true believer in Christ, and I am blessed to know you. I also want to thank Ann, Duane, and Derek Jacobsen, as well as Lois Campagna, for being a part of my life and for your encouraging words and support. I want to thank Al and Pat Gunther for always being loyal friends and being there for me. I also wish to thank Marcia Czech-Miller and Sherry DeGenaro for being wonderful sisters in the Lord who have been cheering me on and giving me confidence that this book would come to its completion.

I want to thank my best friend from college, Dawn Sergi. Dawn, I am grateful that our friendship has endured for all of these years and the gift of my two precious godsons Justin and Jason Sergi. I also want to thank Art Sergi and Brianna Testa. We have been through a lot over the years, which has made our friendship so wonderful.

I am also grateful to Ron Blue and the Kingdom Advisors Program. I also want to thank my course mentor, Sharon Epps, for guiding me through my assignments with Kingdom Advisors. I want to thank Michael Blue, who runs the 9:23 Fellowship.

I want to thank my church family from the Reformed Baptist Church of Lafayette, New Jersey. First and foremost, I want to thank Pastor Patrick Harrison for your steadfast exposition of the Word of God. When I was going through my Certified Kingdom Advisor program, I was grateful that I had your oversight in doing my assignments. I am also thankful for your generosity in reviewing this book's manuscript to maintain its theological accuracy. I also want to thank Sister Sharron Harrison and all the kindness and love you give to our church. I want to thank Pastor Phil Horjus for all your work supporting our church and your great bible studies and Sunday sermons when filling in for Pastor Harrison. I want to thank Jean Horjus for discipling me and taking me under your wings of wisdom. I also want to thank the Bast Family, Tom and Mary Bonney, Patricia Brupbacher, Joan De Groot, Al and Jean Gaines, John Maasbach, Dori Martin, Tom Taylor, Harold Moore, Mildred O'Connell, Carlene Rossi, Nick and Jeanette Van Der Groef, and the Velazquez Family. I also want to thank Alex and Jan Palij for always sharing your life experiences since migrating to this country from Russia and the Czech Republic. Your experiences give you the eyes to see what is happening, and your faith gives you the strength to endure.

Lastly, I want to acknowledge my father, Robert L. Collins (September 15, 1946–January 22, 2022). Dad, you were always my champion who wanted me to get an education. I know you would have been very proud of this book. I only wish you could have lived to see it published.

Theresa J. Yarosh

INTRODUCTION

*"If history could teach us anything, it would be that
private property is inextricably linked with civilization."*
Ludwig von Mises

MANY TODAY ARE questioning what is happening to our country and the world. Many have lived through the dot-com bust, 9/11, and the 2008-2009 financial crisis. The economic upheaval from that crisis left many wondering if what they were doing for their future would be sufficient to sustain their retirement. Then came the latest financial turmoil ushered in with the Covid-19 pandemic. What if I told you that this was a battle from the beginning. What if I told you our economic system had been designed to erode our freedoms. The purpose of this book endeavors to answer those questions and, more importantly, tell you the individuals who have set the course we are now on. Especially since the recent Covid-19 crisis saw unprecedented measures that many, myself included, found both authoritarian and totalitarian. At no point in the history of the world was there a lockdown of society to quarantine healthy individuals and those compromised by a virus. It is normal to quarantine the sick. It is devious to quarantine the healthy in the name of public safety. Observing a coordinated effort to shut down entire countries and their associated economies reveals an insidious agenda.

Ludwig von Mises said, "The middle-of-the-road policy is not an economic system that can last. It is a method for the realization of socialism by installments." The United States of America has seen itself take the middle of the road through various interventions, which were all socialism by stealth. Our nation has been lulled into a consumeristic complacency due to its prosperity. If this nation thrives through its perceived success, we can muddle in the middle. Yet, at the same time, the United States of America finds itself being torn asunder from within. We see attacks on our constitution, civil institutions, and freedoms.

There are stark differences between a biblical worldview and a worldview removed from God. In his book, *The Consequences of Ideas,* R.C. Sproul said, "Not all ideas issue in tangible products. Some ideas are harebrained. Yet even a dreamer's fanciful ideas often become honed into sharp concepts with massive consequences." It is Romans 12:2, which says, "Do not be conformed to this world, but be transformed by the renewal of your mind, that by testing you may discern what is the will of God, what is good and acceptable and perfect." Colossians 2:8 says, "See to it that no one takes you captive by philosophy and empty deceit, according to human tradition, according to the elemental spirits of the world, and not according to Christ." It is the Word of God that guards our hearts and our minds, so we do not fall victim to rogue ideas and philosophies that aim to bind us to despotism, lawlessness, and tyranny.

Perhaps one of the most destructive and malicious of all ideas is utopianism which can be found in the writings of Karl Marx and his *Communist Manifesto*. Marxist ideas and all their mutations have infected economic thought right down to our modern day. History unveils Marxism as a destructive philosophy using Keynesian economics as its method for redistribution of wealth. We could very well be the generation that witnesses that destruction again. Ludwig von Mises, the pioneer of the Austrian School of Economics, wrote that "The Marxian's love of democratic institutions was a stratagem only, a pious fraud for the deception of the masses. Within a socialist community, there is no room left for freedom."

The Austrian School of Economics has always upheld the notion of private property rights and free enterprise and has diligently opposed Marxism in all its forms. In 2020, Rod Dreher wrote the book called *Live Not By Lies*. In it, he said something ominous regarding our current situation. "This totalitarianism won't look like the USSR's. It's not establishing itself through 'hard' means like armed revolution or enforcing itself with gulags. Rather, it exercises control, at least initially, in soft terms. This totalitarianism is therapeutic. It masks its hatred of dissenters from its utopian ideology in the guise of helping and healing." One cannot help but think of the prophetic words uttered by Aldous Huxley during his March 20, 1962, Berkeley Language Center presentation when he said, "There will be, in the next generation or so, a pharmacological method of making people love their servitude, and producing dictatorship without tears, so to speak, producing a kind of painless concentration camp for entire societies, so that people will, in fact, have their liberties taken away from them, but will rather enjoy it, because they will be distracted from any desire to rebel by propaganda or brainwashing, or brainwashing enhanced by pharmacological methods. And this seems to be the final revolution."

We are witnessing a therapeutic form of totalitarianism for the greater good of a society's health and healing through vaccine mandates and passports. If not stopped, these measures can ultimately lead to a social credit score system and a digital currency that could further this tyranny to unprecedented levels in world history. With the assistance of the Federal Reserve, our government is on a spending rampage, the likes of which will result in debt that could never be paid, further mortgaging the future of our citizens. Worse, this may only be the beginning as we see dissenters not being vaccinated sidelined by our society and told that they either comply or lose their livelihood. Countless people are now leaving their jobs both out of principle and desperation for fear that their compliance will lead to other more totalitarian measures. The implications of these job vacancies have not yet been fully translated into economic terms. We see all around us supply chain breakdowns and questions regarding our own Federal Reserve Chairman for his stock trading activities due to others involved with the Federal Reserve who are being investigated for insider trading. Those in many economic circles speculate that it is the goal of certain individuals in power to take over the Federal Reserve to facilitate the endless printing of money, which could lay the foundation for universal basic income all as a result of the mindless servitude we now find ourselves living in.

This age-old struggle has been since the beginning of time. Since the words uttered in the Garden of Eden, "Did God really say," (Genesis 3:1-5), the pages of history have revealed a battlefield that is for the minds of those who fall victim to godless ideas and philosophies that lead entire societies astray. This includes the theories of economics. For those who seek a global totalitarian dictatorship, the only way to manifest their ideology is through controlling the world's commerce and currencies. Yet, for those who study the Bible and history, this current method of control exercised through the pandemic is merely a modern-day method of forcing Marxist ideas upon us. It is the virus of communism that has infected both the minds of unsuspecting fools and societies at large.

It is lamentable when reflecting upon those who fled to the shores of North America to escape totalitarianism only to find it kicking the door down and standing in their living rooms. We are being hypnotized by television and social media propaganda and are falling victim to unapologetic censorship. What tragedy befalls us all in this generation as we see the Great Economic Deception weaponized against our freedoms. And yet it is within our power under the authority of God to restore what is true based not only on the Constitution of the United States of America but on the Constitution of Heaven, which is the Word of God that influences our free will under a Sovereign God who gives us true freedom.

"The struggle for freedom is ultimately not resistance to autocrats or oligarchs but resistance to the despotism of public opinion."
Ludwig von Mises

THE FINANCIAL CRISIS OF 33 AD

*"But when the fullness of time had come, God sent forth his Son,
born of woman, born under the law, to redeem those who were
under the law, so that we might receive adoption as sons."*

Galatians 4:4-5

MANY CHRISTIANS DO not take the time to research the economic and political climate that occurred during the life and crucifixion of Jesus Christ. What we will learn from this chapter is the political and economic climate during the time that Jesus walked this earth are no different from our own especially during our present Covid-19 crisis. We must remember there are always biblical solutions no matter what situation we may find ourselves.

Biblical scholars generally date the crucifixion of Christ around 33 AD, the same year that Rome was contending with a significant financial crisis. As with many economic crises, there is a related chain of events. The same is true of the financial crisis of 33 AD. In addition, there was a political crisis during this period of time involving a plot to overthrow Emperor Tiberius as well as the execution of the perpetrator Lucius Aelius Sejanus. To fully understand this chain reaction, we will quote at great length from the economic historian Otto C. Lightner's book *A History of Business Depressions. Lightner writes the following:*

"The year 33 AD was full of events in the ancient world. It marked two disturbances as the outgrowth of the mob spirit. The first was in the remote province of Judea, where one Christus was tried before Pontius Pilate, was crucified, dead, and buried. The other event was the great

Roman panic which shook the empire from end to end. The consternation accompanying the latter died down, and it was soon forgotten, but the murmurings of the former swept down the centuries until, bursting into flames, it enveloped the world. A description of the panic reads like one of our own times: the important firm of Seuthes & Son of Alexandria was facing difficulties because of the loss of three richly laden spice ships in a Red Sea storm, followed by a fall in the value of Ostrich feathers and Ivory. About the same time a great house of Malchus & Co., of Tyre, with branches in Antioch and Ephesus, suddenly became bankrupt as a result of a strike among their Phoenician workmen and the embezzlements of a freedman manager. These failures affected the Roman Banking house of Quintus Maximus and Luvius Vibo. A run commenced on their bank and spread to other banking houses that were said to be involved, particularly the Brothers Pittius. The Via Sacra was the Wall Street of Rome, and this thoroughfare was teeming with excited merchants. These two firms looked to other bankers for aid, the same as is done in modern days, but unfortunately at this time an outbreak had occurred among the semi-civilized people of North Gaul, where a great deal of Roman capital had been invested, and a moratorium had been declared by the government on account of the disturbed conditions. Other bankers, fearing the suspended conditions, refused to aid the first two houses and this augmented the crisis."

Before we continue with the financial crisis of 33 AD, we must now refer to another ominous event that was unfolding at that time. Emperor Tiberius, who was living on the Island of Capri, became aware in 31 AD that Lucius Aelius Sejanus was plotting to overthrow him. Sejanus started as a soldier and became the Prefect of the Praetorian Guard. The Praetorian Guard was the elite force that constituted the Emperor's bodyguards. As time went on, Sejanus became a confidant of Emperor Tiberius. Sejanus was a man of selfish ambition and a spirit of covetousness. He wanted to ascend the throne and be the Emperor of the Roman Empire. In addition, Sejanus had political allies in both the Roman Senate and the financial sector of Rome. As a result of Sejanus's betrayal, Emperor

Tiberius secretly shifted power away from Sejanus to another loyalist of his within the Praetorian Guard. Tiberius then ordered the arrest of Sejanus after which he began his reign of terror. Sejanus, his family, and the Roman senators conspiring against the Emperor were found and executed. These individuals would be considered Non-Amicus Caesaris—No Friend of Caesar. As a result, land owned by those found to be traitors was sold, causing land prices to drop. As these land prices fell, agriculture declined, leading to a credit crisis.

We now return to Lightner's book on the history of business depressions. Lightner says, "Money was tight for another reason: agriculture had been on the decline for some years, and Tiberius had proclaimed that one-third of every Senator's fortune must be invested in lands within the province of Italy in order to recoup their agricultural production. Publius Spinther, a wealthy nobleman, was at that time obliged to raise money to comply with the order and had called upon his bank, Balbus Ollius, for 30,000,000 sesterces, which he had deposited with them. This firm immediately closed their doors and entered bankruptcy before the praetor. The panic was fast spreading throughout all the provinces of Rome and the civilized world. News came of the failure of the great Corinthian bank, Leucippus' Sons, followed within a few days by a strong banking house in Carthage. By this time all the surviving banks on the Via Sacra had suspended payment to the depositors. Two banks in Lyons next were obliged to suspend; likewise, another in Byzantium. From all provincial towns creditors ran to bankers and debtors with cries of keen distress only to be met with an answer of failure or bankruptcy. The legal rate of interest in Rome was then 12 percent and this rose beyond bounds. The praetor's court was filled with creditors demanding the auctioning of the debtors' property and slaves; valuable villas were sold for trifles, and many men were reputed to be rich and of large fortune were reduced to pauperism. This condition existed not only in Rome, but throughout the empire. Gracchus, the praetor, who saw the calamity threatening the very foundation of all the commerce and industry of the empire, dispatched a message to the Emperor, Tiberius, in his villa at Capri. The merchants waited breathlessly for four days until the courier returned. The Senate assembled quickly while a vast throng, slaves and millionaires, elbow to elbow, waited in the forum outside for tidings of the Emperor's action. The letter was read to the Senate, then to the forum as a breath of relief swept over the waiting multitude. Tiberius was a wise ruler and solved the problem with his usual good sense. He suspended temporarily the processes of debt and distributed 100,000,000 sesterces from the imperial treasury to the solvent bankers to be loaned to needy debtors without interest for three years. Following this action the panic in Alexandria, Carthage, and Corinth quieted."

Lightner's analysis of this ancient financial crisis is akin to the 2008 financial crisis. In 2008, there was a mortgage crisis that led to a real estate bust. This in turn led to a credit crisis that had to be quelled by something called Quantitative Easing. Quantitative easing involves the lowering of interest rates to stabilize the economy. Before Ben Bernanke and John Maynard Keynes, Tiberius and his zero interest rate program appeared to stabilize the empire. Many historians contend that Rome was at its peak under Tiberius. What unfolded over time were many waves of financial panic; bread and circuses (not unlike our modern-day welfare programs), debt peonage like our modern-day credit oligarchy, and the debasement of their currency like our modern-day Keynesian inflationary policies.

In Judea, another crisis was forming. We have an allusion to this crisis in Matthew 21:12-13, "And Jesus entered the temple and drove out all who sold and bought in the temple, and he overturned the tables of the money-changers and the seats of those who sold pigeons. He said to them, 'It is written, "My house shall be called a house of prayer," but you make it a den of robbers.'" Jesus was confronting the corruption of the Elite of Jerusalem. In his book *The Temple*, Alfred Edersheim writes the following: "The total sum derived annually from the Temple tribute has been computed at about 76,000 pounds. As the bankers were allowed to charge a silver meah, or about one-fourth of a denar on every half-shekel, their profits must have amounted to nearly 9,500 pounds, or deducting a small sum for exceptional cases, in which the meah was not to be charged, say about 9,000 pounds—a very large sum." Edersheim continues saying, "It must therefore have been a very powerful interest which Jesus attacked, when in the Court of the Temple He poured out the changers money, and overthrew the tables, while at the same time He placed Himself in direct antagonism to the sanctioned arrangements of the Sanhedrin, whom He virtually charged with profanity." In addition, scholars including Edersheim have stated that this was a mandatory tithe. This tithe does not appear to be an issue since it benefits the poor. However, this tithe was often done under coercion, including severe beatings to extract payment. This was a form of extortion. Worse still, this was a nationalized tithe entrusted to the Temple Elites to care for the poor. However, did they? Perhaps this is why Jesus said to them the poor will always be with you because the Temple Elite were not interested in the poor at all but lining their own coffers or Jesus was simply citing Deuteronomy 15:11 which states "For there will never cease to be poor in the land. Therefore I command you, 'You shall open wide your hand to your brother, to the needy and to the poor, in your land."

Further confrontations between Jesus and the corrupt leaders would lead the ruling elite of Jerusalem to plot against Him. They found a willing candidate in Judas Iscariot who would betray Jesus for thirty pieces of silver, the price of a dead slave. We read in Exodus 21:32, "If the ox gores a slave, male or female, the owner shall give to their master thirty shekels of silver, and the ox shall be stoned." We further read of this betrayal in Matthew 26:14-16, "Then one of the twelve, whose name was Judas Iscariot, went to the chief priests and said, "What will you give me if I deliver him over to you?" And they paid him thirty pieces of silver. And from that moment he sought an opportunity to betray him."

A mob was gathering, and the mob demanded the crucifixion of Jesus. However, the custom of the time was to release a prisoner during the Feast of Passover. Pontius Pilate gave the crowd a choice between Jesus and a notorious criminal Barabbas. It should be noted that it was in Pontius Pilate's best interest to execute Barabbas because he was an insurrectionist and was therefore deemed an enemy of Rome. However, the crowd intimidated Pilate with the accusation that he was no friend of Caesar. On the surface, this seems to be no threat since Pontius Pilate was a ruthless man who brutally treated the people of Judea. So why did Pilate cave to this allegation of being no friend of Caesar and crucify Jesus Christ? Could it be because his political benefactor was none other than Sejanus? Sejanus was executed for being no friend of Caesar. This severe threat could imperil Pilate with Rome and entangle him in Tiberius's reign of terror.

What we see in this account is stunning. We refer back to one quote from Lightner's book that says, "The important firm of Seuthes & Son of Alexandria was facing difficulties because of the loss of three richly laden spice ships in a Red Sea storm, followed by a fall in the value of Ostrich feathers and Ivory." Matthew 8:23-27 clearly communicates that even the winds and the sea obey their Creator God. Concerning Tiberius and Sejanus, Daniel 2:21 clearly communicates that kings and rulers are established and removed by the Sovereign God.

If people think that our situation today due to the Covid-19 pandemic is hopeless, we must understand that Jesus lived during a very volatile time in history. All too often individuals will seek out worldly solutions whether by politicians or economists only to find them lacking instead of turning to the truth of the Word of God. In John 18:37-40 we read, "Then Pilate said to him, 'So you are a king?' Jesus answered, 'You say that I am a king. For this purpose I was born and for this purpose I have come into the world—to bear witness to the truth. Everyone who is of the truth listens to my voice.' Pilate said to him, 'What is truth?' After he had said this, he went back outside to the Jews and told them, 'I find no guilt in him.'" Later, Pilate ordered the Crucifixion of Jesus Christ.

We see the Providence of God in the sinking of the ships and a chain reaction of economic events; we see the failed attempt by Sejanas to overthrow Tiberius. We see Pontius Pilate's position leading to his decision to crucify Jesus. Rome and Judea were in a state of anxiety and panic, both financially and politically. The Elite power of Rome and Judea was on the line.

Pontius Pilate stood face to face with God Incarnate, the Way, the Truth, and the Life (John 14:6), and before Jesus could answer his question, Pilate walked away. Countless men and women have similarly walked away from the truth of God, especially during economic and political upheaval and in this we see a reflection of our sinful human nature. In summary it was a financial crisis and government corruption in Rome and Judea that became the catalyst for the most liberating victory the world has ever known—The Death and Resurrection of the Lord Jesus Christ!

The King of Kings and the Lord of Lords
was betrayed for the price of a dead slave.

THE QUESTION OF OWNERSHIP

*"Private property is both a gift and a certain type of power God
has entrusted to humanity as stewards. It was God's intention that
mortals should be equipped with this gift and power and that
under God, they should exercise dominion over the earth."*
Dr. Walter C. Kaiser, Jr.—Old Testament scholar

To UNDERSTAND THE Great Economic Deception we find ourselves in, we must first and foremost start at the beginning of time. Also, we will be asking and answering the question: "Is God a Socialist?" We will also be exploring the worldview of Karl Marx, John Maynard Keynes, Thomas Piketty, and Klaus Schwab. However, before we can delve into the topics above, we must first answer the question of ownership. The foundational concept of ownership is what determines the ability to acquire private property. However, where did the construct of acquiring private property emerge?

If we turn to scripture, we find the following verses; Psalm 24:1-2, "The earth is the Lord's and the fullness thereof, the world and those who dwell therein, for he has founded it upon the seas and established it upon the rivers." 1 Corinthians 10:26, "For the earth is the Lord's, and all it contains." Haggai 2:8, "The silver is Mine, and the gold is Mine,' declares the Lord of hosts." Psalm 50:10, "For every beast of the forest is Mine, The cattle on a thousand hills." Many Christians acknowledge the biblical worldview that "God owns it all". However, few understand the implications of this ownership. The foundation of all economic theory should be the simple verse, "And then God created the Heavens and the Earth."

Dr. Walter C. Kaiser, Jr., a distinguished Old Testament scholar, develops this theme in his paper *Ownership and Property In the Old Testament Economy. Kaiser writes,*

"It was at creation that God the Creator committed the world and its resources to humanity (Gen. 1:28–29). It was because the man and the woman were made in the image of God that they were commanded to subdue the created order and to exercise dominion over the whole of it. As a result, God **granted dominion** to this first human pair under his law, but he **did not grant his sovereignty** to them, for God alone is Lord and the only sovereign over all." Therefore, we conclude that God is the grantor. We are the beneficiaries. His expectation is that we will manage and steward these resources based on His Laws, Principles, and Statutes.

God retains sovereign ownership because, as the Creator of the heavens and the earth, it is His private property, as shown in the verses we referenced at the beginning of this chapter. To further solidify this granted dominion to man, a system of tithes and offerings was established. Since God designed the earth to yield to man by his productivity, the first fruits of that production would be given back to God as a way of calibrating man's mind and spirit to the proper functioning of God's economy. The system becomes an ever-expanding cycle by acknowledging God through tithes and offerings.

As part of this cycle and according to God's design, we develop virtues such as industriousness, resilience, wisdom, and insight as a way to acquire private property. All aspects of our work are also gifts from God. We are conduits of God's resources to benefit the world. Each image-bearer of God expands their creativity on earth because we have been granted dominion to do so. This becomes the bedrock of a well-functioning capitalistic system. John Calvin viewed private property as being essential to the social order. A well-functioning market economy requires property rights to ensure that all goods and resources are used efficiently. Self-interested individuals will use the property at their disposal in such a way as to maximize business profits and household stewardship. The ability to receive a return on your property provides additional incentives. This can only be productive when man exercises his stewardship responsibilities to God, the Creator.

This capitalistic system becomes corrupted when man, because of his alienation from God, determines that sovereign ownership is now his, removed from God's laws, principles, and statutes. Here we find tyrants squelching the free will of mankind and robbing from them their God-given right to acquire private property. This is a catastrophic inversion of God's intended social order founded upon dominion granted from God to human beings. This leads to authoritarian tyranny by individuals or elite groups seeking to usurp all production for themselves. These, in turn, extract the first fruits of its production by corruption, fraud, taxation, overbearing regulations, theft, and even violence disrupting the cycle because God is now removed and replaced by man. Through the mechanism of government and man-made laws, man devises a vicious cycle of reduced productivity built on the premise of scarcity. From this scarcity, the redistribution of seized property occurs, further reducing production. The objective is to cut man off from the Creator and all the God-given virtues within the human soul. Where there was resilience, there is now despair. Where there was diligence, there is now sloth. Where there was wisdom, there is now madness. Where there was insight, there is now resignation and conformity to the false gods of state tyranny, established through envy, rebellion, and theft.

We read in Isaiah 14:12-14 the following, "How you are fallen from heaven, O Lucifer, son of the morning! How you are cut down to the ground, You who weakened the nations! For you have said in your heart: 'I will ascend into heaven, I will exalt my throne above the stars of God; I will also sit on the mount of the congregation on the farthest sides of the north; I will ascend above the heights of the clouds, I will be like the Most High.'"

Since the beginning of earth's history, Lucifer has been waging a destructive battle for sovereignty over the heavens and the earth. Because of his envious pride, he desired to steal God's ownership of private property for himself (Isaiah 14:12-15). All tyranny throughout history comes down to the issue of ownership. Yet the scriptures make it clear "God owns it all". Anything to the contrary is a deception distorting the virtuous cycle of the gift of dominion to humanity.

In our next chapter, we will determine if God granting dominion of the earth to man means He is a socialist who wants redistribution of wealth.

IS GOD A SOCIALIST?

*"I would not have you exchange the Gold of Individual Christianity
for the Base Metal of Christian Socialism."*
Charles Spurgeon

*"Socialism is a philosophy of failure, the creed
of ignorance, and the Gospel of Envy."*
Winston Churchill

THIS CHAPTER IS of significant importance, and it is especially critical in light of what we hear concerning inequality, social justice, and the redistribution of wealth schemes imposed upon us.

In 1 John 4:1, God instructs His children, "Beloved, do not believe every spirit, but test the spirits to see whether they are from God, for many false prophets have gone out into the world." In His love, He warns His followers to test everything that we encounter in this world against the Word of God to determine its veracity or its deceitful nature.

As we read in our previous chapter, the answer as to whether or not God is a Socialist and a Social Justice Warrior comes down to the question of ownership and the use of acquired private property. From a biblical worldview, it is understood that "God owns it all" and has granted dominion of the earth to man but not His Sovereignty. Ephesians 2:10 says, "For we are his workmanship, created in Christ Jesus for good works, which God prepared beforehand, that we should walk in them." God molded within each individual their purpose, calling, and economic position in life.

Before we continue, we would like to define the word Sovereignty. The Sovereignty of God is the Christian teaching that God is the supreme authority, and all things are under His control. Easton's Bible Dictionary defines God's Sovereignty as His "absolute right to do all things according to His own good pleasure." This includes the ability for man to acquire private property for his personal use and perpetuate the Kingdom of God. In conformity with the idea of Biblical Sovereignty, it was God's Will to send His Son to this earth.

Karl Marx called for the abolition of private property and called for state ownership of the means of production. Therefore, Karl Marx, an atheist who did not believe in God nor His Sovereignty, sought that Sovereignty for himself and his partners in crime. We hear the words of Winston Churchill declaring Karl Marx as the Chief Architect of the Gospel of Envy. Communism and Socialism are antithetical to God's Supreme Authority and Control. Communism and Socialism seek to concentrate all power and control in the hands of an Elite few who pull the levers of government and production. Communism destroys the free markets and, more importantly, creates a welfare state that severs the inalienable rights bestowed on us by God the Creator.

The mechanism of this stealth takeover involves leveraging sinful human nature rooted in greed and envy. Alexis de Tocqueville said, "I have a passionate love for liberty, law, and respect for rights. Liberty is my foremost passion. But one also finds in the human heart a depraved taste for equality, which impels the weak to want to bring the strong down to their level, and which reduces men to preferring equality in servitude to inequality in freedom. **Equality is a slogan based on envy.** It signifies in the heart Nobody is going to occupy a place higher than I." Because of man's alienation from God and his rebellion against God, we see nothing new under the sun as regards tyranny over his fellow man and the desire for man to consolidate his power and control over others as though he is God.

We will now expand on the implications of communism and socialism on a society as a result of man's alienation from God and his acting as though he is God. Leviticus 18:21, says, "You shall not give any of your children to offer them to **Molech**, and so profane the name of your God: I am the Lord." In his book, *God vs. Socialism*, Joel McDurmon writes the following in his section on Kings and Total Sacrifice. "In the Samuel passage, the Hebrew uses the standard word for 'king'—mlk, or Melech. This common word appears all through the Old Testament, but when referring to a particular practice of neighboring pagan divine-king States, the Hebrew scribes replaced the vowels with those from the Hebrew word boseth, 'shame.' The resulting name **Molech** refers to the pagan total-State, the great tyrannies incurred where **the civil State usurped the place of God and worship in society** and demanded the ultimate sacrifice." Whether the average person believes it or not, every single day, our children are being sacrificed to **Molech**. This is manifested through Socialist ideas and practices that seek to usurp the place of God in our lives.

One of the more disturbing ideas that we are contending with involves Jesus Christ as Social Justice Warrior and Master Redistributionist of Wealth. Before we continue, we would like to point out that over 2,350 verses in the Bible pertain to money and stewardship. Also, Jesus Christ in the New Testament spoke more about money than He did regarding Heaven and Hell. Because of this, many see His words admonishing the rich as the platform for which social justice and redistribution of wealth must occur, claiming that this type of thinking is Christian. What few seek to do is put the words of Jesus Christ into a 33 AD historical context. Failing to do so can cause the reader of the New Testament Scriptures to divorce Jesus from His economy.

Doug Stuart, CEO of the Libertarian Christian Institute, explains the following: "The New Testament was written during a time with a very different economic and sociopolitical situation from our own. Being rich in the first century was not due to free-market engagement in highly productive enterprises, but from being part of the **privileged class where labor was exploited in the ugliest of ways**. Nor was being poor about having a lousy work ethic or random misfortune. Economic status was not as fluid as in free markets; people could not just 'move up the ladder,' and widespread economic growth did not depend on open markets as we have in capitalism. So, of course, under **conditions of exploitation** (not voluntary exchange), we would expect nothing less than for Jesus to give warnings to that **type of rich person!**"

Also, the economist Jerry Bowyer emphasized this point on the weekly radio show called *A Neighbor's Choice* when he said, "The anti-wealth passages in the New Testament are always in the **context of state exploitation of the poor**. Jesus never, anywhere in the Gospels, confronts a single person in entrepreneurial Galilee, where he was from, about wealth. All of his confrontations about wealth occur after he goes down to Judea, which is the political capital of that ancient region."

What is quite ironic is that many Socialists use specific passages of scripture and ones that Jesus spoke admonishing the rich as justification for social equity and justice and redistribution of wealth. They do not realize that the Son of God is delivering His message to them. They are the ones who seek to confiscate, tax, regulate, and redistribute wealth for their benefit under the guise of helping the poor and disadvantaged. They are the ones who seek centralized power and control, creating their own **Molech State**.

It should now be clear that God is not a Socialist. He is against human control through subjugation and authoritarian tyranny by using an economic system that perverts His Will.

Our next chapter will demonstrate that collectivism was attempted very early in our nation's founding and abandoned for an economic structure based on the Biblical Principles of private property.

THE PILGRIM EXPERIMENT
IN COLLECTIVISM

"The society we have described can never grow into a reality or see the light of day, and there will be no end to the troubles of states, or indeed, of humanity itself, till philosophers become rulers in this world, or till those, we now call kings and rulers really and truly become philosophers, and political power and philosophy thus come into the same hands."
Plato—The Republic (375 BC)

"The philosopher whose dealings are with divine order himself acquires the characteristics of order and divinity."
Plato—The Republic (375 BC)

THIS CHAPTER WILL explore how Plato's worldview and influence nearly stopped the progress of freedom and liberty based on private property ownership. To demonstrate this, we must go back in time to the United States of America's formative years. November 11, 2020, marked the 400th anniversary of the Mayflower reaching the shores of Plymouth. William Bradford, Governor of the Colony, said, "As one small candle may light a thousand, so the light here kindled hath shone unto many, yea in some sort to our whole nation." The journey of the Mayflower began in England in July of 1620. However, because her sister ship, the Speedwell was unseaworthy, the Mayflower did not formally set sail for Virginia until September 6, 1620.

The Separatists were headed to Jamestown, Virginia, a colony from 1609 to 1610. The Mayflower, although heading for Jamestown, was blown off course and landed in Cape Cod on November 11, 1620. A few weeks later, they sailed up the coast to Plymouth and built their colony. Of 102 passengers who embarked on this voyage of freedom within a few months, fifty-one of these courageous God-fearing souls had died.

Today we call these colonists the "Pilgrims"; however, they did not get that name until 1669. These people were English Separatists fleeing religious persecution under King James I of England. These Separatists were escaping the age-old conflict of man-made government and rulership. They were escaping kings' rule whereby the government was a counterfeit god demanding the worship of the Church of England with an iron fist. The rule of certain people over others is found in the worldview and influence of Plato and his work called *The Republic*. We will learn that Plato was the one whose work would influence the idea of the Rule of Kings and communal living (Socialism). This philosophy influenced the Mayflower voyage investors who would seek a return on their investment through a collective structure or, as William Bradford called it, the common course.

Before Karl Marx, there was Plato, who believed in the idea of Central Planning over the masses. In Plato's *The Republic*, there would be two classes of people: those who govern and those governed. He also felt that rulers must beget rulers, which essentially was a form of selective breeding. Furthermore, Plato advocated that the State must own property and that all production, labor, raw materials, and finance should be nationalized. Plato in *The Republic* writes, "Both the community of property and the community of families, as I am saying, tend to make them more truly guardians; they will not tear the city in pieces by differing about 'mine' and 'not mine;' each man dragging any acquisition which he has made into a separate house of his own, where he has a separate wife and children and private pleasures and pains; but all will be affected as far as may be by the same pleasures and pains because they are all of one opinion about what is near and dear to them, and therefore they all tend towards a common end."

Plato in *The Republic* developed the idea of a utopian city-state ruled by a Philosopher King. Also, the word utopia means an imagined place or state where everything is perfect. Therefore, we can surmise that since we live in a fractured creation with fallen human beings alienated from God, the actual definition of utopia is no place on earth. It is a fantasy that leads to tyranny when individuals or groups feel the need to rule over others to create a perceived paradise from their own depraved minds. This utopia is for themselves, while others are deemed irrelevant and need to be contained and controlled through private property confiscation.

Many have contended that the Separatists who landed in Plymouth in 1620 were exploited by the "Investors" of the day like the failed colony in Jamestown. However, these "Investors" could be seen as modern-day Venture Capitalists taking a risk and even more so after Jamestown's failure. Because these were investors, they were seeking a return on their investment. To do this, they structured the colony in the form of shared ownership. The terms of the agreement were that everything at the end of seven years would be **equally** divided between the investors and the colonists. Therefore, this structure would secure their investment because the colonists were 3,000 miles away with no oversight.

In essence, it was not the greed of the capitalists who exploited the Pilgrims but a socialist planned economy that nearly led to the entire colony's starvation. Herein lies the hazard of removing private property ownership from any economic system. It should also be noted that the people who came to Plymouth were godly men and women. Under the heavy yoke of a communal structure, the colony witnessed a moral, spiritual, and societal collapse.

William Bradford wrote the following assessment of their experiment with communal property; "Community of property was found to breed **much confusion and discontent**, and **retard much employment** which would have been to the general benefit. ... For young men who were most able and fit for service objected to being forced to spend their time and strength **working for other men's wives and children, without any recompense.** ... The strong man or the resourceful man had no more share of food, clothes, etc., than the weak man who was not able to do a quarter the other could. **This was thought injustice.** ... The aged and graver men, who were ranked and equalized in labor, food, clothes, etc., with the humbler and younger ones, thought it some **indignity and disrespect** to them. ... As for men's wives who were obliged to do service for other men, such as cooking, washing their clothes, etc., they considered it a **kind of slavery,** and many husbands would not brook it." Also, William Bradford noted that there was envy, strife, and thievery, especially since the planted crops were beginning to fail due to the collective structure they were living under.

As we can see, a socialist planned economy leads to confusion, discontent, reduced employment, envy, strife, thievery, injustice, indignity, disrespect, lack of incentive, the destruction of individual liberty, near starvation, and a state-run program of slavery. The Pilgrims were enslaved to an economic structure based on the worldview of investors influenced by Plato. Plato was the original Central Planner and Philosopher King, born an Aristocrat whose very birthright entitled him to rule the masses of those who needed to be governed by his self-professed **divinity**. In Plato's own words, he said, "The philosopher whose dealings are with divine order himself acquires the characteristics of order and divinity."

Man has always desired to be like God, subjecting others to their reprobate lusts of power and control even under the guise of a utopian world that does not exist. Only God's intended economic system built on private property can unleash the invisible hand of commerce to liberate an individual under God's authority. As flawed as Capitalism may seem, it is only flawed due to man's fallen sin nature and alienation from God. However, it maintains the heart of private property rights that guarantees freedom and liberty despite man's inherent flaws.

In our next chapter, we will reveal what the celebration of Thanksgiving was all about.

"The failure of that experiment of communal service, which was tried for several years, and by good and honest men, proves the emptiness of the theory of Plato and other ancients, applauded by some of later times, that the taking away of private property, and the possession of it in community, by a commonwealth, would make a state happy and flourishing; as if they are wiser than God."
William Bradford—Of Plymouth Plantation

"The true creator is necessity, who is the mother of our invention."
Plato—*The Republic*

THE CELEBRATION OF
PRIVATE PROPERTY RIGHTS

"Though I bequeath you no estate, I leave you in the enjoyment of liberty."
Governor William Bradford—Plymouth

*"The utopian schemes of leveling are arbitrary, despotic,
and in our government unconstitutional."*
Samuel Adams

*"The moment the idea is admitted into a society that property is
not as sacred as the Laws of God and that there is not a force of Law
and public justice to protect it, anarchy and tyranny commence.
If 'thou shalt not covet' and 'thou shalt not steal' were not
commandments of heaven, they must be made inviolable precepts
in every society before it can be civilized and made free."*
John Adams, 1768

Our last chapter demonstrated the failure of a communal structure that led to the near-starvation of Plymouth's entire colony. This starvation resulted from failing crops due to food rationing because of the socialist economy the colonists lived in. When the shipwreck known as socialism comes to a nation's shores, it is a sure path to the extinction of the masses by way of starvation.

This chapter will now shed light on what the celebration of Thanksgiving was all about. Governor William Bradford was faced with what seemed to be an impossible situation as the colony was collapsing and would meet a devastating end due to limited food. Because William Bradford was a Puritan Separatist, he knew the Word of God. Also, Governor William Bradford was influenced by the work and worldview of the French lawyer, economist, historian, and philosopher Jean Bodin (1530-1596). Bodin's work called the *Six Books of the Commonwealth* was found in Bradford's library. In the works of Jean Bodin, he lays out the foundation of the state, a republic where private property is an inalienable right. Jean Bodin is quoted as saying, "Sharing out of the goods of others is the theft under the banner of equality." Jean Bodin also wrote that "of all the causes of sedition and changes in the Republic, there is none greater than the excessive wealth of a few subjects, and the extreme poverty of the majority."

In the spring of 1623, at the behest of Governor William Bradford, the colony implemented a new economic system influenced by the Word of God and the writings of Jean Bodin. At this critical juncture in the colony's history, every family was assigned their own private parcel of land. They were all responsible for their own crops, which would be used to feed their own families. At this fateful moment in time, the invisible hand of capitalism ushered in economic incentives. William Bradford writes, "God in His Wisdom saw that another plan of life was fitter for them." He also said that the changed order of their colony "Was very successful. It made all hands very industrious so that much more corn was planted than otherwise would have been by any means the Governor or any other could devise, and saved him a great deal of trouble, and gave far better satisfaction." As a result of the private property initiative, the Pilgrims had more than they could share, which is why they invited the Indians to the harvest. The first Thanksgiving in 1621 was not a cornucopia of collectivism; it was a celebration of Private Property Rights that gave birth to the United States of America's founding. The colony was so thriving that the Pilgrims set up trading posts, exchanged goods with the Indians, and paid off their debt to the investors who bankrolled their journey to America. By 1624, the Pilgrims were now exporting corn by boatloads.

William Bradford, in 1647, wrote on the Autumn of 1623 by saying, "By this time harvest was come, and instead of famine now God gave them plenty, and the effect of their particular planting was well seen, for all had, one way and other, pretty well to bring the year about, and some of the abler sort and more industrious had to spare, and sell to others; so as any general want or famine hath not been amongst them since to this day."

It has already been 400 years since the Mayflower Compact and the Pilgrims, giving birth to a courageous nation. This was a nation that saw its Declaration of Independence and Constitution built on the Word of God. In recent years, we have been invaded from within by academic ideologues whose goal of communism is to take power away from the people and enslave us like the kings of a bygone age. Abraham Lincoln said, "America will never be destroyed from the outside. If we falter and lose our freedom, it will be because we destroyed ourselves." We must ask ourselves how many years are left of this Great Republic. Our Flag stood in defiance of those who sought to destroy this nation built on the Word of God. The blood of those who died cry out from the ground seeking justice for this nation. How long do we turn from these threats? How long do we let our comforts imprison us? These comforts give us over to complacency that leads to destruction. We must hold on to this nation like Governor William Bradford with everything we have or face a slow death of all our freedoms and liberties and starvation of our rights one by one.

As Thanksgiving comes every year, let us not forget the Mayflower. May we all remember William Bradford, the Governor of Plymouth. It was the courage of the Mayflower's men and women who set foot on the ship of dreams that would alter the world's destiny. Those who come to our shores have visions of freedom in their minds in hopes of experiencing liberty and bear with patience the hardships they encounter for the sake of their children, just as the Pilgrims did. Freedom is not easy, for it is fought and won by those who know tyranny. We have seen the pictures of so many ships of dreams which came through New York's Harbor as those immigrants looked with tears in their eyes when they first saw the Statue of Liberty; the words from Emma Lazarus comfort them when she says;

> *"Give me your tired, your poor,*
> *Your huddled masses yearning to breathe free,*
> *The wretched refuse of your teeming shore.*
> *Send these, the homeless, tempest-tost to me,*
> *I lift my lamp beside the golden door!"*

The Word of God opened the golden door to those men and women before us, like William Bradford. We have entered only by the Grace of God through His Word that fashioned freedom through our Constitution. Let us hold on to it for future generations and never let it go.

> *"Proclaim LIBERTY Throughout All the*
> *Land Unto All the Inhabitants thereof."*
> Liberty Bell's inscription (Leviticus 25:10)

THE LUCIFERIAN PILLARS OF MARXISM

"My people are destroyed for lack of knowledge;
because thou hast rejected knowledge, I will reject thee."
Hosea 4:6 (KJV)

"A collective tyrant spread over the length and breadth of the land,
is no more acceptable than a single tyrant ensconced on his throne."
Georges Clemenceau

"Equality may exist only amongst slaves."
Aristotle

B EFORE WE DELVE into the key figures who have distorted our eco-
nomic system, we would like to address two critical figures in the
Bible, Pharaoh and Nimrod. They demonstrate the foundations of the
Luciferian Pillars of Marxism and all of its Satanic mutations.

We now turn to the Book of Genesis and the story of Joseph and
Pharaoh. It all begins with how Joseph interpreted the dream of Pharaoh
regarding the fat and lean cows. The lean cows would represent a great
famine on the lands. Joseph would instruct the people to give one-fifth of
all the harvest to be stored for what was to come. From Genesis 47:13-19,
we read, "Now there was no food in all the land, for the famine was very
severe, so that the land of Egypt and the land of Canaan languished by
reason of the famine. And Joseph gathered up all the money that was
found in the land of Egypt and in the land of Canaan, in exchange for the
grain that they bought. And Joseph brought the money into Pharaoh's
house. And when the money was all spent in the land of Egypt and in

the land of Canaan, all the Egyptians came to Joseph and said, 'Give us food. Why should we die before your eyes? For our money is gone.' And Joseph answered, 'Give your livestock, and I will give you food in exchange for your livestock, if your money is gone.' So they brought their livestock to Joseph, and Joseph gave them food in exchange for the horses, the flocks, the herds, and the donkeys. He supplied them with food in exchange for all their livestock that year. And when that year was ended, they came to him the following year and said to him, 'We will not hide from my lord that our money is all spent. The herds of livestock are my lord's. There is nothing left in the sight of my lord but our bodies and our land. Why should we die before your eyes, both we and our land? **Buy us and our land for food, and we with our land will be servants to Pharaoh.** And give us seed that we may live and not die, and that the land may not be desolate.' ... So when the famine had spread over all the land, Joseph opened all the storehouses and sold to the Egyptians, for the famine was severe in the land of Egypt. Moreover, all the earth came to Egypt to Joseph to buy grain, because the famine was severe over all the earth."

In Genesis 47:23-25, we read, "Then Joseph said to the people, 'Behold, I have this day **bought you** and your land for Pharaoh. Now here is seed for you, and you shall sow the land. And at the harvests, you shall give a fifth to Pharaoh, and four-fifths shall be your own, as seed for the field and as food for yourselves and your households, and as food for your little ones.' And they said, '**You have saved our lives**; may it please my lord, we will be **servants to Pharaoh.**'"

Joel McDurmon, in his book *God versus Socialism*, states the following; "The 'government salvation in crisis' theme has a precedent in the story of Egypt. The lesson is simple: crisis or not, when government becomes the means of provision, the result can only be loss for the people." In his book *The Naked Socialist*, Paul B. Skousen writes, "The surest path to dictatorship is braced with the promises of universal care." Also, Frederic Bastiat said, "Socialism, like the ancient ideas from which it springs, confuses the distinction between government and society. As a result of this, every time we object to a thing being done by the government, the socialists conclude we object to its being done at all. We disapprove of state education. Then the socialists say that we are opposed to any education. We object to state religion. Then the socialists say we want no religion at all. We object to state-enforced equality. Then they say we are against equality. And so on, and so on. It is as if the socialists were to accuse us of not wanting persons to eat because we do not want the State to raise grain."

No matter what the crisis may be, famine, pestilence, pandemics, natural disasters, financial panics, planes flying into buildings unleashing the specter of war, all serve a purpose. Those in power invoke legislative intervention, which leads to the destruction of individual freedom and liberty, all under the deception of humanity's universal care.

Now we turn our attention to another biblical character named Nimrod. Nimrod comes from the Hebrew verb "marad," which means to rebel. Adding the m changes the meaning to the rebel, or we will revolt. Nimrod was the original Communist provocateur inspired by Satan. From Genesis 10:9-10, we read, "He was a mighty hunter before the Lord. Therefore it is said, 'Like Nimrod, a mighty hunter before the Lord.' The beginning of his kingdom was Babel, Erech, Accad, and Calneh, in the land of Shinar." In his book *The Naked Socialist*, Paul B. Skousen writes that "Ancient writers said Nimrod turned the people from God, telling them that true joy came not from the Lord, but by their own hand. He instituted pagan worship, idolatry, and the worship of fire. He changed the government and put himself in charge, essentially declaring himself to be god. He forced the people to become dependent on him for every-thing they required—an ancient version of today's food stamps, pensions, and general government welfare. Genesis says Nimrod's reign of tyranny and force was ultimately conquered by the confusion of tongues at the Tower of Babel when all the people were scattered for lack of a common language or understanding."

In an interesting commentary by Matthew Henry, he says the fol-lowing as it pertains to Nimrod. "Under the pretense of hunting, he gathered men under his command, in pursuit of another game he had to play, which was to make himself master of the country and to bring them into subjection. He was a mighty hunter, that is, he was a **violent invader** of his neighbors' **rights and properties**, and a persecutor of innocent men, carrying all before him, and endeavoring to make all his own by **force and violence.**" In another commentary on Nimrod, Matthew Henry writes, "It does not appear that he had any right to rule by birth but either his fitness for government recommended him, as some think, to an **election,** or by **power and policy** he **advanced gradually,** and perhaps insensibly, into the throne. The antiquity of civil government, and particularly that form of it which lodges the **sovereignty in a single person.** If Nimrod and his neighbors began, other nations soon learned to incorporate under one head for their **common safety and welfare.**" Frederic Bastiat said, "It is impossible to introduce into society a greater change and a greater evil than this: conversion **of the law into an instrument of plunder.**"

In his book, *The Naked Socialist,* Paul B. Skousen writes that "Socialism stands atop seven pillars of control rooted in the power and authority of Ruler's Law." They are as follows:

1. All-powerful RULERS
2. A society divided into CASTES and CLASSES
3. All things in COMMON
4. All things REGULATED
5. Compliance is by FORCE
6. Control of INFORMATION
7. NO INALIENABLE RIGHTS

Karl Marx and Friedrich Engels contrived a Luciferian ten-point plan to alter Capitalism's social order built upon granting the earth's dominion through a Sovereign God's private property. Friedrich Engels said that the summation of the Communist Manifesto was the abolition of private property. Karl Marx was the Nimrod of the Modern Age.

Below is a summation of the Luciferian Pillars of Marxism:

1. Abolition of private property
2. A heavy progressive and graduated Income tax
3. Abolition of all rights of inheritance
4. Confiscation of all property of emigrants and rebels
5. Centralization of credit in the hands of the State, utilizing a national (central) bank with State Capital and an exclusive monopoly
6. Centralized communication and transport in the hands of the State
7. Extension of Factories and Instruments of production owned by the State
8. Equal obligation of all to work
9. Gradual abolition of all distinction between town and country by a more equitable distribution of the population over the country
10. Free Education for all children in public schools

The influence of the worldview of Karl Marx is one of the most tragic we have seen in our most recent history. To this day, its influence has penetrated our macroeconomic system through John Maynard Keynes and even our Government and Educational System. It was a gradual infiltration through stealth that has leveled an enormous blow to this country. It all starts with the removal of God from society. Vladimir Lenin wrote, "We must combat religion—this is the ABC of materialism and consequently of Marxism." The only way out of Marxism's demonic and seducing spirit is to restore our nation to its foundation built by those with a biblical worldview.

> *"When virtue suffers neglect and death, the historian knows an end to the whole is not far behind."*
> Paul B. Skousen

> *"Take no part in the unfruitful works of darkness, but instead expose them. For we are not contending with flesh and*

blood, but against the principalities, against the powers,
against the world of rulers of this present darkness, against
the spiritual hosts of wickedness in the heavenly places."
Ephesians 5:11, 6:12

WHO WAS KARL MARX?

"Men start revolutionary changes for reasons
connected with their private lives."
Aristotle

"Words I teach all mixed up into a devilish muddle. Thus anyone
may think just what he chooses to think. With disdain, I throw my
gauntlet full in the face of the world. And see the collapse of this
pygmy giant whose fall will not stifle my ardor. Then will I wander
godlike and victorious through the ruins of the world. And giving
my words an active force, I will feel equal to the creator."
Human Pride—Poem by Karl Marx

"My soul, once true to God, is chosen for Hell."
Karl Marx

W E WILL NOW turn our attention to one of the most destructive individuals the world has seen in the modern age. He is the Father of
Communist lies, and his ideology enshrined in his Communist Manifesto
has been responsible for the violent carnage that has killed an estimated
150 million people. With his pernicious philosophical partner Friedrich
Engels, he would give birth to some twentieth-century monsters. These
monsters include Vladimir Lenin, Joseph Stalin, Mao Zedong, Zhou
Enlai, Kim il-Sung, Ho Chi Minh, Pol Pot, Nikita Khrushchev, Fidel
Castro, Che Guevara, Josip Broz Tito, Nicolae Ceaușescu, and Mikhail
Gorbachev. Even today, some Marxists roam amongst us who do not
fully understand the foundation of these hellish philosophies.

Now we must remove the scales from our eyes. We must see the real influence of Socialism and Communism. We must analyze the ideology of a man who was an academic derelict and an intellectual vagabond. We cannot turn ourselves away from his perverse preoccupation with the Devil and hell, which alarmed his father and those around him. With great furor, Marx would write as the proletariat's pride-filled philosopher and the new world order economist. For example, Friedrich Engels captures the true nature of Karl Marx by writing the following about him: "Who comes rushing in, impetuous and wild. Dark fellow from Trier, in fury, raging. Nor walks nor skips, but leaps upon his prey in tearing rage, as one who leaps to grasp broad spaces of the sky and drag them down to earth. Stretching his arms wide open to the heavens. His evil fist is clenched, he roars interminably as though ten thousand devils had him by the hair." Further, we quote an address to Marx in a letter dated August 1844 from his wife, Jenny von Westphalen, "Your last pastoral letter, high priest, and bishop of souls has again given quiet rest and peace to your poor sheep." Marx was a mad social scientist whose Luciferian ideas regarding human nature would destroy entire societies through ungodly upheaval, usurpation of authority, starvation, imprisonment, and death, all in the name of equality, social justice, and redistribution of wealth. The implications of denying God are found in Psalm 14:1-7, "The fool says in his heart, 'There is no God.' They are corrupt, they do abominable deeds; there is none who does good. The Lord looks down from heaven on the children of man, to see if there are any who understand, who seek after God. They have all turned aside; together they have become corrupt; there is none who does good, not even one. Have they no knowledge, all the evildoers who eat up my people as they eat bread and do not call upon the Lord? There they are in great terror, for God is with the generation of the righteous. You would shame the plans of the poor, but the Lord is his refuge. Oh, that salvation for Israel would come out of Zion! When the Lord restores the fortunes of his people, let Jacob rejoice, let Israel be glad."

Few know the background of the young Karl Marx, his early poetic writings, and his play "Oulanem," let alone his real personality. In one of his poems, Karl writes the following: "Look now, my blood-dark sword shall stab, unerringly within my soul. God neither knows nor honors art. The hellish vapors rise and fill the brain, Till I go mad and my heart is utterly changed. See the sword—the Prince of Darkness sold it to me. For he beats the time and gives the sign. Ever more boldly, I play the dance of death." In a romantic ballad titled "Nocturnal Love," Marx seems fascinated with poisoned cups and the flames of hell. In his play "Oulanem," the choice of this title leaves one realizing something quite sinister. If one were to research this name, it is now associated with Anti-Christ. Marx writes in scene three of "Oulanem," "All lost! The hour is now expired, and time Stands still. This pigmy universe collapses. Soon I shall clasp Eternity and howl, Humanity's giant curse into its ear. Eternity! It is eternal pain, death inconceivable, immeasurable. An evil artifice contrived to taunt us."

Interestingly, Marx uses the word pigmy. One of the phrases pigmy uses is to describe an insignificant or unimpressive person—an intellectual pigmy. Perhaps this is what he thought of those around him, or he may have thought this about himself and, in turn, sought to tear down those whom he deemed significant and impressive. Paul Johnson, the author of the book *Intellectuals*, says the following about the poetic writings of Karl Marx, "Savagery is a characteristic note of his verse, together with the intense pessimism of the human condition, hatred, a fascination with corruption and violence, suicide pacts and pacts with the devil."

On May 5th, 1818, Karl Marx was born in Trier, Prussia, which was a German Confederation. He was ethnically Jewish and, more importantly, from devout Rabbinic families on both sides. His father's family had supplied Trier's rabbis since 1723. The Marx family converted to Christianity by the end of 1819 due to social pressures involving Anti-Semitism. The Marx family would be considered upper middle class by today's standards. At the age of seventeen, Marx went to the University of Bonn, studying philosophy and literature. However, because his father was a lawyer, he wanted his son to pursue a law career. This caused contention between father and son. In 1836, Karl Marx became engaged to Jenny von Westphalen and enrolled in the University of Berlin to study law. At this point, Marx was introduced to and influenced by the writings of Georg Wilhelm Friedrich Hegel, who had died on November 14, 1831. The work of Hegel was much debated in the philosophical circles in Europe. In his book, *The Devil and Karl Marx*, Paul Kengor writes that Hegel "taught that history is a series of struggles between opposing forces, with each successive struggle unfolding on a progressively higher plane than the one that preceded it." Ultimately, according to Hegel, human history is a dialectical unfolding truth—that is, "Truth" itself. Hegel was a Christian. As one Hegel scholar wrote, this "dialectical unfolding ends in the revelation of God." Hegel was an ideational dialectic. Marx's plane was not based on the battle of ideas—the so-called "ideational plane" of Hegel—but on economics, classes and materialism. It was "dialectical materialism." At this juncture, Marx was a professed Atheist.

In the 1840s, Marx met another Atheist associate named Mikhail Bakunin in Paris. Bakunin was an admirer of Marx. Bakunin wrote the book *God and State*, and in it, he said, "If God really existed, it would be necessary to abolish Him." He also wrote that Satan was "the eternal rebel, the first free thinker and emancipator of the worlds." There is no doubt that Karl Marx smirked a sardonic grin at the thought of God being abolished and Satan being the emancipator of worlds. It must have ignited the hellish vapors in his brain into a raging fire. After all, it was Karl Marx who would say that religion is the opium of the people.

As we can see, Marx was inspired by dark occultic ideas that were antithetical to faith in God. For our Christian readers, this harks back to the Garden of Eden when Satan said, "Did God really say?" It is the ancient rebellion of man against God. It is the desire of a fallen creature to become like God and seek worship for himself. The idea we can become gods and goddesses leads to absolute tyranny when a mere human being with a fallen sin nature seeks to control others and make them their slaves in mind, body, and spirit. This is the hidden truth of Marxism. Karl Marx was a man who was fascinated with the Devil's workings, and in turn, he was his vessel for all that would subject the world to the dominion of hell and not what God granted to man that would bring a virtuous cycle that leads to eternal life. In all its forms, Marxism leads to the death of mind, body, and spirit.

The Devil does indeed prowl around like a roaring lion looking for someone to devour. He sets his demonic gaze on those with the lowest moral character to magnify their selfishness, greed, and envy, turning them into his agents. Karl Marx became the agent provocateur to complete Satan's specter of severing humanity from God. Karl Marx said, "The idea of God is the keynote of a perverted civilization. It must be destroyed."

"I long to take vengeance on the One who rules from above."
Karl Marx

In our next chapter, we will look at the sad state of affairs of the Marx household under the jobless husband and father Karl Marx and his penchant for racism.

KARL MARX—DISCONNECTED "FAMILY" MAN AND RACIST

"But if anyone does not provide for his relatives, and especially for members of his household, he has denied the faith and is worse than an unbeliever."
1 Timothy 5:8

"Every day my wife says she wishes she and the children were safely in their graves, and I really cannot blame her, for the humiliations, torments and alarums that one has to go through in such a situation are indeed indescribable."
Letter from Karl Marx to Friedrich Engels

TO FURTHER UNDERSTAND the depraved mind of Karl Marx, we would now like to turn our attention to one of the most tragic aspects of his life as it pertains to his wife and children. Karl Marx married Jenny von Westphalen in June of 1843. The Champion of the Proletariat spent most of his life with his wife and children in miserable squalor, relying on friends and family for financial support, including his partner in crime, Friedrich Engels. Many biographers of Karl Marx report that he would be drunk at times, did not bathe, and was an unkempt slob. He did not work, which put tremendous strain on his wife, Jenny. Jenny was coerced into his extractor of others' wealth as a beggar asking family and friends for money and warding off bill collectors and mitigating eviction and auction of their possessions. As one can surmise, this had a severe impact on their children, as we shall learn.

Karl Marx, who sought to abolish any inheritance in his tenets of Communism, made continuous attempts to receive an early inheritance, including demands placed upon his mother for a $6,000 advance. What seemed to work for Mr. Marx did not work for the Bourgeois class of people he disdained. The State should take their legacy to their children, but his inheritance was another matter.

It is even more disturbing that Karl and Jenny made sure their children were raised as Atheists. Sadly, when his children asked their father about the story of Christmas and what it meant, he said that Jesus Christ was a poor carpenter who wealthy men killed. Imagine all around the Marx children the Christmas lights, the good cheer, and all the songs sung to the Lord Jesus Christ only to be told about wealthy murderers who desired the death of a carpenter from Galilee. As if this was not bad enough, Karl had more in store to terrorize his children's young minds. When the family lived in London, Karl would take his children for walks on Sunday. While other families went to church, Karl Marx would tell his children the story of a magician and toymaker named Hans Rockle, who made a pact with the devil, and there was no escaping it. Imagine their young minds trying to absorb a toymaker involved with the devil. Perhaps this was Karl's story of himself as he fashioned himself as the magician and toymaker of the world whose toys involved weapons of mass destruction resulting from a pact he made with the devil. There was no way out for Karl, for he crossed the point where his own conscience became seared by his own hatred of God. Two of Karl's daughters committed suicide, and one of them did so under a suicide pact with her husband.

One of the most distressing and tragic periods for the Marx family was between 1848 and 1850. The Marx family lived like wandering refugees between Brussels, Paris, Cologne, and London. They moved to boarding houses wherever they could find them. During this time, there was a frigid winter season, and the newest Marx child named Heinrich died before his first birthday due to the terrible conditions that Jenny and her children were forced to live in. Paul Johnson writes in his book Intellectuals, "Jenny left a despairing account of those days from which her spirits, and her affections for Karl Marx never really recovered." In 1855, tragedy struck again in the Marx household when their eight-year-old son Edgar, the apple of Karl's eye, died in his arms from intestinal tuberculosis. The reason was due to the unhealthy living conditions in which the Marx children were raised. Karl Marx's fury was unleashed at this juncture as he wrote his second tome of evil revelations, *Das Capital*, against the Bourgeois. According to Marx, disease resulting from deprivation had killed two of his children. Yet, this disease and deprivation leading to death were none other than a mirror image of Karl's nature reflected to him.

The Provocateur of the Proletariat, Karl Marx, did not even consider getting a job to support his wife and children. He was too busy smoking cheap cigars and writing his depraved plans of Communism to extract wealth from those who did support their families. To help the Marx family due to Karl's blatant irresponsible self-induced misery upon his own family, Jenny's mother sent a nanny to help them. Helene Demuth, whose nickname was Lenchen, was a childhood friend of Jenny. On the surface, this appears to comfort Jenny since she was falling into despair and illness. Although Lenchen worked for the Marx family, she received no pay from Karl Marx and was treated as an "indentured servant." One biographer of Karl Marx wrote that Lenchen was Karl's "Chattel to be exploited unmercifully." Perhaps, he was practicing his Communist ideas on her even though she was a working-class woman. Lenchen was the closest thing Karl had ever gotten to the "Proletariat," to which he sought to invoke a revolution against the Bourgeois class. What is truly fascinating is that Karl Marx accused the Bourgeois class of doing what he did to Lenchen.

Eventually, in another horrific betrayal of his wife, Karl made Lenchen pregnant. One biographer wrote, "Marx was seeking a sexual receptacle in Lenchen. She was virtually his bond slave was a matter of entire indifference to him." In June of 1851, Lenchen gave birth to a baby boy. Karl denied that he was the father and refused any financial support. Sadly, the boy eventually named Freddie was sent into foster care. Friedrich

Engels, Karl's partner in all things, Communism, and a known womanizer, accepted paternity for the child to save Karl's failing marriage. On Friedrich Engels's death bed, he admitted that Freddie was Karl Marx's son.

Many biographers have speculated whether or not Karl raped or seduced Lenchen. However, based on Marx's writings, it has been revealed that there have been many passages concerning rape, which has led many to conclude that Karl Marx repeatedly raped Lenchen resulting in her pregnancy. Karl Marx even said to Friedrich Engels, "Blessed is the man with no family," and he looked down upon women. Marx openly professed his desire to have sons and said of his wife Jenny to Friedrich Engels, "My wife, alas, has delivered a girl and not a boy," he lamented that Jenny had "deficient birthing abilities."

In addition to his views on women, Karl Marx was a vehement racist who would direct his angry, hate-filled epithets toward blacks and Jews. Marx even wrote an essay in 1844 called *On The Jewish Question*, where he stated, "What is the worldly cult of the Jews? Haggling. What is his worldly god? Money. Very well! Emancipation from haggling and money, and thus from real Judaism, would be the self-emancipation of our age." What is truly ironic is that Karl Marx treated money as his god with his dialectical materialism, and distorted economics to create class warfare. Since Karl Marx was both an Atheist and an admirer of Charles Darwin, it is painful to see how these comments and others like them would be used years after his death to inspire none other than Adolf Hitler to go on his murderous rampage of the Jews.

It is now that we must pause and consider the worldview of a man named Karl Marx. A man who took to fits of drunkenness was an unkempt jobless slob, disdained women, said "blessed is the man with no family," was irresponsible and reckless in his support of his children, was a racist against blacks and Jews, and a possible rapist. Is it any wonder that when his worldview starts "revolutions," we see the most hellish behavior emerge in our society. This includes destroying the family, invoking hatred and violence by those who do not work against those who do. It all culminates with the rape of all of our freedoms and liberty, leaving us chattel to be exploited unmercifully like indentured servants to the State. What happened to Karl Marx's family and Lenchen would be played out on the world stage, destroying the lives of millions, and, like the poor carpenter from Galilee, their fate would be death.

In the Sermon on the Mount, the poor carpenter from Galilee, who is the Son of God, said in Matthew 5: "Blessed are the poor in spirit, for theirs is the kingdom of heaven. Blessed are those who mourn, for they shall be comforted. Blessed are the meek, for they shall inherit the earth. Blessed are those who hunger and thirst for righteousness, for they shall be satisfied. Blessed are the merciful, for they shall receive mercy. Blessed are the pure in heart, for they shall see God. Blessed are the peacemakers, for they shall be called sons of God. Blessed are those who are persecuted for righteousness' sake, for theirs is the kingdom of heaven. Blessed are you when others revile you and persecute you and utter all kinds of evil against you falsely on my account."

Karl Marx's battle was far beyond a poor carpenter from Galilee. Like Lucifer, his struggle was against God Himself in his sordid attempts to wrest away the rightful owner of private property and to distort God's natural order of economics. Sadly, this would only be the beginning as his depraved ideas would influence another economist who would use a form of stealth Bolshevism all under the guise of capitalism.

WHO WAS JOHN MAYNARD KEYNES?

*"A worldview is like a Grand 'Master Gear,' moving all the other
'Gears' that form and fashion any society. At its core, a worldview
is a person's 'Big Picture' of ultimate reality, as shaped by
subconscious assumptions and conscious beliefs about five critical
issues: God, Creation, Humanity, Moral Order and Purpose."*
Dr. Christian Overman—Assumptions that Affect our Lives

*"Too often, we excuse those who are willing to build
their lives on the shattered dreams of others."*
Robert F. Kennedy

WE WILL NOW turn our attention toward a discussion of our economic condition. Few realize that an economist from the 1930s
has influenced our current state of financial affairs. As a nation, we see
trillions of dollars in federal stimulus, expanded money supply growth,
and overt manipulation of interest rates designed to debase our very currency. Very much like the Fall of Rome, we are on a dangerous trajectory.

Few people realize that much of modern economic theory resides
with the economist John Maynard Keynes. Keynes wrote the signature
book *The General Theory of Employment, Interest, and Money* published
in 1936. Because of the influence of Keynes, our global economic system
has come to embrace his theories without knowing the worldview inherent in his thinking. Now the question becomes, does the thinking and
worldview of an economist who died in 1946 matter today?

Simply put, worldview matters. Dr. Christian Overman, in his book
Assumptions that Affect our Lives, wrote, "We often underestimate the

importance of unspoken assumptions behind the words and visible actions of those around us. Like an iceberg floating in the ocean with just ten percent visible above the waves and ninety percent below the surface, we sometimes lose sight of the fact that the words we hear and read, and the actions of others that we see, are first shaped by invisible thoughts, deep in the unseen world of the heart."

To understand the economic trajectory we find ourselves on, we must now direct our attention to the mind and actions of John Maynard Keynes. For starters, in 1903, Keynes became a member of the Cambridge Apostles in Great Britain. This group was an "intellectual elite" interested in philosophy and its applications to aesthetics and life. Keynes emerged as the leader of this hermetic society with his homosexual lover Giles Lytton Strachey. The clarion call of this society's arrogance was that the Society (Cambridge Apostles) was "real." In contrast, the rest of the world is only "phenomenal," meaning that the rest of the world was less substantial and less worthy of attention. To further complicate matters, John Maynard Keynes viewed homosexuality as superior to heterosexuality. Also, he had a deep-seated hatred and utter contempt for the values and virtues of the middle class, for conventional morality, for savings and thrift, and the primary institutions of family life.

In 1909, Keynes became involved in the Bloomsbury group consisting of eclectic members involving themselves in literature, philosophy, and culture. Further, a key influence on John Maynard Keynes was the philosopher G.E. Moore. Interestingly, Keynes adopted from the philosopher what he termed "Moore's religion" involving personal ethics while rejecting Moore's social ethics that he framed to be Moore's morals. As a result of this à la carte menu of thought, Keynes wrote in a startling 1938 paper the following:

"In our opinion, one of the greatest advantages of his [Moore's] religion was that it made morals unnecessary. We entirely repudiated a personal liability on us to obey general rules. We claimed the right to judge every individual case on its merits, and the wisdom to do so successfully. This was a very important part of our faith, violently and aggressively held, and for the outer world, it was our most obvious and dangerous characteristic. We repudiated entirely customary morals, conventions, and traditional wisdom. We were, that is to say, in the strict sense of the term, immoralists."

In addition, to Keynes's views about morality or lack thereof, the researcher Zygmund Dobbs, who wrote the book *Keynes at Harvard*, said, "Keynes always ready to guide others freely advised his fellow debauchees to go to Tunis 'where bed and boy' were also not expensive."

The question many are asking at this point is, how did someone with this worldview come into prominence in the world of economics? From his book *Keynes the Man*, Murray Rothbard gives us the answer: "Part of the reason, as the economist Joseph Schumpeter has pointed out, is that governments, as well as the intellectual climate of the 1930s, were ripe for such conversion. Governments are always seeking new sources of revenue and new ways to spend money, often with no little desperation. Yet, economic science for over a century had sourly warned against inflation and deficit spending, even in times of recession."

The stage was set for John Maynard Keynes, the monetary alchemist and Platonian philosopher-king, to advise America's first Communist Czar Franklin Delano Roosevelt. John Maynard Keynes was the architect of modern inflationary policies that, like ancient Rome, are profitable to governments and not the citizens. These very same policies are being deployed as we see trillions of dollars of stimulus spending utilized to quell the ongoing damage of our current economic crisis due to the Covid-19 Pandemic.

It should be evident that worldview does matter and has profound long-term implications. John Maynard Keynes was an immoralist, a homosexual, advocated for pedophilia, had hatred and contempt for middle-class values, including conventional morality, savings, thrift, and basic family life.

With a worldview such as this from the "Cambridge Apostles" darling, what could possibly go wrong with our economic system? I contend with just about everything. Our next chapter will reveal that Keynes was not a capitalist but a Bolshevik operative.

> *"See to it that no one takes you captive by philosophy and empty deceit, according to human tradition, according to the elemental spirits of the world, and not according to Christ."*
> Colossians 2:8 (ESV)

THE BUOYANTLY BOLSHEVIK
JOHN MAYNARD KEYNES

"My Christmas thoughts are that a further prolongation of the war, with the turn things have taken, probably means the disappearance of the social order we have known hitherto. With some regrets, I think I am on the whole, not sorry. The abolition of the rich will be rather a comfort and serve them right anyhow. Well, the only course open to me is to be buoyantly Bolshevik; and as I lie in bed in the morning, I reflect with a good deal of satisfaction that, because our rulers are as incompetent as they are mad and wicked, one particular era of a particular kind of a civilization is very nearly over."
John Maynard Keynes's Letter to his Mother—1917

"Within him are the seeds of rebellion."
R. F. Harrod—Official Biographer of John Maynard Keynes

"Keynes is a socialist that does not believe in the family"
Clarence W. Barron—1918

"We are all socialists now."
Sir William Harcourt

SINCE WORLDVIEW IS essential to our thinking, we would now like to demonstrate that Keynesian Economic Theory is nothing more than an economic deception to promote the political movement of global communism. This political deception started long ago under the Fabian Society. American Fabianism began as early as 1887, and like a virus, has infected many of our institutions of higher learning. The Keynesian theory of economics has saturated the academic world and is considered unprecedented in modern times. Keynesian economics started its prominence at Harvard University. From Harvard, this Bolshevik virus has infected Yale, Princeton, the University of Chicago, the University of Wisconsin, the Massachusetts Institute of Technology, and almost every college and university in the United States of America. Because Keynesianism was the primary method of economic theory taught in academia, the graduates of this political deception would then take this Bolshevik virus into various government departments, including the State Department, the Presidential office, the Treasury, the Department of Agriculture, and the Department of Labor.

By 1913, John Maynard Keynes, through his association with Fabian Socialists such as Sidney Webb, A. C. Pigou, and Alfred Marshall, began to promote eliminating the gold standard, which was at the foundation of the monetary system of the global economy. In exchange for eliminating the gold standard would be a "managed currency." A managed currency allows for State-Socialism, and the Fabian Socialists had espoused this idea since the turn of the century. Also, John Maynard Keynes influenced Franklin Delano Roosevelt twenty years later to begin taking the United States of America off of the gold standard. When Franklin Delano Roosevelt began the process of taking the United States off the gold standard in 1933, John Maynard Keynes wrote in the London Daily Mail (June 1933) that "President Roosevelt is Magnificently Right," and Keynes added that Roosevelt's policies "lead to the managed currency of the future."

To continue, we must understand the significance of a managed currency and its application to our present Covid-19 crisis condition. From the book "Keynes at Harvard" is the following quote, "For years it had been a point of Socialist Strategy that complete government control of currency and all money and currency values is a chief lever in moving society toward **redistribution of wealth and complete Socialism**." To achieve complete Socialism, you must also undermine private enterprise to lead the way toward nationalism, as was seen in Communist Russia and Fascist Germany and Italy.

John Maynard Keynes, in the Yale Review of 1933, wrote his feelings on the subject of private enterprise; "The decadent international but individualistic capitalism, in the hands of which we found ourselves after the war, is not a success, it is not intelligent, it is not beautiful, it is not just, it is not virtuous—and it does not deliver the goods. In short, we dislike it and are beginning to **despise** it."

At this point, we must now turn our attention to another significant individual who was the Chief Propagandist for Socialism in the United States of America. Stuart Chase was an American Economist, a Fabian Socialist, and a 1910 graduate of Harvard University. He wrote the book *A New Deal*, published in 1932. Franklin Delano Roosevelt took this title to frame the Socialist Slogan for his administration. Stuart Chase would celebrate that John Maynard Keynes was the "**unofficial President of the United States.**"

Again from *Keynes at Harvard*, we quote the following: "Keynesianism secured the blessing of President Franklin Delano Roosevelt. Pandora's Box was now open. Not only the socialists but communist agents and spies plus opportunists and careerists of all stripes climbed on the Keynesianism bandwagon. The socialists discreetly avoided mentioning that Keynes and the Keynesian theories were merely clever facades to cover the conquest by Fabian socialism of an unsuspecting population." Once again, we turn to Stuart Chase, who said, "Mr. Keynes, following **Karl Marx**, used the great corporation as an institution increasingly ripe for state control or **outright ownership**. He finds many parallels with the state trusts of Soviet Russia."

And from the book *Keynes at Harvard*, we find one of the most sobering of quotes "Traditional left-wing demands for greater constitutional rights actually disguise a plot to do away with the present Constitution altogether. Stuart Chase and other Keynesian agitators have questioned the fundamental validity of the Constitution of the United States. **Chase has advised his readers that the Constitution is 'outmoded' and should** be scrapped in favor of a 'more effective federal control' and 'to circumvent the old doctrine of checks and balances, by setting up boards and commissions which, like the Federal Trade Commission, combine legislative, judicial and administrative powers.' This matches the Keynesian concept of a strong Central Government without checks and balances, which in effect would allow one bureaucratic body to be policeman, judge, jury, and executioner."

It should be self-evident from this quote that the Keynesian formula, resulting from its Bolshevik nature, fits all totalitarian ideologies. Sadly, history bears the proof of this claim. Mussolini was very fond of John Maynard Keynes. The Nazi Fascists were wildly enthusiastic supporters of John Maynard Keynes. Juan Peron's dictatorship of Argentina used Keynesian techniques as the authority on economic and political matters. Right down to taking over the United States of America in a silent Bolshevik coup by ushering in the New Deal under Roosevelt, which now seems to be reaching its zenith under the Global Green New Deal. Yet, the failure of Socialism and Totalitarianism litter the pages of history books, letting us see the fate that lies before us if we do not return to the original intended foundation of this country.

True liberty and freedom come from the Word of God. All forms of Totalitarianism are opposed to the Word of God. All tyrants rise from the ashes of a debased mind handed over to itself. Like John Maynard Keynes, within them are the seeds of rebellion. William Ames—a Puritan, wrote, "Ownership and differences in the amount of possessions are ordinances of God and approved by Him."

> *"The rich and the poor meet together;*
> *the Lord is the Maker of them all."*
> Proverbs 22:2 (ESV)

John Robinson was the Puritan Pastor of the Pilgrim Fathers before they left on the Mayflower. He commented, "God could…either have made men's states equal, or have given everyone sufficient of his own.

But he hath rather chosen to make some rich, and some poor, that one might stand in need of another, and help another, that so he might try the goodness and mercy of them who are able, in supplying the wants of the rest."

We hear in the media that we are at war with an invisible enemy. That invisible enemy is the rise of modern-day Totalitarian Czars and Technocrats. They are using the Bolshevik framework of economics established long ago to usher in a One World Government and Global Communism. Our next chapter will reveal the insidious nature and philosophical dangers of the Fabian Society.

THE FABIAN SOCIETY

"I also made it quite clear that Socialism means equality of income or nothing, and that under Socialism, you would not be allowed to be poor. You would be forcibly fed, clothed, lodged, taught, and employed whether you liked it or not. If it were discovered that you had not character and industry enough to be worth all this trouble, you might be executed in a kindly manner; but whilst you were permitted to live you would have to live well."
George Bernard Shaw—Intelligent Woman's Guide to Socialism

"However [political parties] may now and then answer popular ends, they are likely in the course of time and things, to become potent engines, by which cunning, ambitious, and unprincipled men will be enabled to subvert the power of the people and to usurp for themselves the reins of government, destroying afterwards the very engines which have lifted them to unjust dominion."
George Washington

I predict future happiness for Americans, if they can prevent the government from wasting the labors of the people under the pretense of taking care of them."
Thomas Jefferson

THIS CHAPTER AIMS to demonstrate what influenced the worldview of John Maynard Keynes. It will be quite evident that Keynes was a trained Marxist, and his economic policies would alter global economics for generations to come.

We must start at the beginning on January 4, 1884, in Great Britain, when the Fabian Society was born. The Fabian Society was a covert group of Socialists who worked to infiltrate society without being detected for what they indeed were—Marxists. They derived their name in honor of the Roman general Quintus Fabius Maximus Verrucosus (nicknamed Cunctator, meaning the "Delayer"). Inside of the group's first pamphlet, it declared, "For the right moment you must wait, as Fabius did most patiently when warring against Hannibal, though many censured his delays; but when the time comes you must strike hard, as Fabius did, or your waiting will be in vain, and fruitless."

Early in the group's formation, they used a significant symbol of their organization. It was a Wolf in Sheep's Clothing.

Because of the obvious connotations of the Wolf in Sheep's Clothing, it was abandoned. According to author Jon Perdue, "The logo of the Fabian Society, a tortoise, represented the group's predilection for a slow, imperceptible transition to socialism, while its coat of arms, a 'wolf in sheep's clothing,' represented its preferred methodology for achieving its goal."

Many know the story of the tortoise and the hare. The tortoise won the race because of its slow and methodical plodding to achieve its goal. The same way the Fabian Society has infiltrated every aspect of our culture to achieve its singular purpose—A Marxist Revolution without bloodshed.

The Fabian Society found several interesting people amongst its ranks. They included George Bernard Shaw, H.G. Wells, and Bertrand Russell. Another member of note is John Neville Keynes, the father of John Maynard Keynes. While at Cambridge University, the elder Keynes wrote the book *The Scope and Method of Political Economy* (1890). What is striking about this book is how the elder Keynes writes against the notion of private enterprise. Is it any wonder the younger Keynes would write the book *The End of Laissez-Faire* in 1926 against the idea of private enterprise? Like his father, John Maynard Keynes was a member of the Fabian Society.

Also, there were two very influential people involved in the Fabian Society: Sidney and Beatrice Webb. It should be stressed that there was a connection between the Fabian Society and none other than Vladimir Lenin that dates back to 1897. Vladimir Lenin translated Sidney Webb's Fabian publication "History of Trade Unionism." Margaret Cole, who was a Socialist politician and writer, wrote: "The name of Sidney Webb had an almost mystical prestige in the Russian Communist Party since it was his 'History of Trade Unionism' which Lenin had read and translated during his exile and which he had recommended to all Party members." The Bolsheviks were considered Comrades by the Fabians.

In 1932, Sidney and Beatrice Webb visited Soviet Russia. When they returned from their Communist field trip, they published a book in 1935 called *Soviet Communism—A New Civilization*. As it turns out, the entire book had been prepared in the Soviet Foreign Office. In addition, John Maynard Keynes's signature book *The General Theory* was published in 1936. Because of his involvement in the Fabian Society, his book is nothing less than a Marxist fraud masquerading as "Economics."

Before we continue, we must stress the utter deviousness of the Fabians and what their ultimate goals have been since their inception.

From Fabian News, London, June 1892, they contend the following: "A cover of respectability and good manners as a means of gaining entry into all social activities while avoiding the use of the label 'socialism,' promoting Socialism continuously by coloring such activities with new terms so as to attain **Socialism by stealth**."

From the book *Keynes at Harvard* is the following: "The Fabians, under the leadership of such economists as Sidney Webb, J.A. Hobson, Alfred Marshall, A. C. Pigou and John Maynard Keynes have dissected, analyzed, charted and evaluated statistically (with their own particular slant) every facet of private enterprise. They insist that society inevitably leads to Socialism as a replacement for our present economic and political systems." John Maynard Keynes is considered the Father of Macroeconomic Theory, and it is his theories that the world economy has been utilizing since he came into prominence. He was groomed for a specific moment in history, which was to infiltrate the central banking mechanisms of the world with Marxist ideology.

We want to add some insightful revelations by Rose Martin. Rose Martin wrote the book called *Fabian Freeway High Road to Socialism in the USA*. This prophetic book documents the rise and progress of Socialism in Britain and the United States and tells the story of the many early triumphs of the philosophy of **socialist incrementalism** known as Fabian Socialism. Published on July 17, 1966, Rose Martin emphasizes

Fabian influences on Woodrow Wilson and Franklin Delano Roosevelt (America's First Communist Czar) and continues the discussion through the 1960s, when the book initially appeared. Here we want to demonstrate the desire of the Fabian Society to overthrow Christianity and what they thought of Christians in general.

"The inference seemed to be that, since Christians were not overly bright, they could easily be led down the garden path to Socialism by a false appeal to ideals of brotherhood and **social justice**. To churchgoers among the voting population, Sidney Webb had reasoned shrewdly; Socialist goals must be presented cautiously—in terms that did not appear to conflict with their religious beliefs. For the most part, its spokesmen prudently avoided outraging the beliefs of religious-minded persons, while soliciting their support for Socialist candidates and persons."

Further. Rose Martin writes, "In the Fabian Socialist movement, as in Soviet Marxism, there was always a strong element of political messianism, diametrically opposed to the religious messianism of One who proclaimed: 'My Kingdom is not of this world.' Both Socialist and Communist literature stress the supposedly communal character of early Christianity, undetectable to anyone familiar with the Epistles of St. Paul. Revolutionary Marxism, open or disguised, was presented as being the 'Christianity of today.' Voluntary charity and renunciation of one's own goods were confused with the forcible confiscation of other people's property; as illustrated in the famous phrase of John Maynard Keynes, 'the euthanasia of the rentier,' that is, the mercy-killing or painless extinction of those who live on income from invested capital."

In no more than 137 years, the Fabian strategy has been enormously successful. Both Britain and the United States are heavily regulated and heavily taxed societies with highly socialized economies where government agents exercise vast control over the movement of **capital and currency** through a sizable bureaucratic system.

Fabian Socialism is no longer incrementalism but a saturation of our society that has bewitched us all. The Covid-19 pandemic has seen the Central Bank and Government move into a more authoritarian state of control, the likes of which have never been seen in the United States of America. We must heed the prophetic words of our founding father Thomas Jefferson when he said: "I sincerely believe that banking establishments are **more dangerous** than standing armies and that the principle of spending money to be paid by posterity, under the name of funding, is but **swindling futurity on a large scale.**" We cannot look toward bankers or to governments for our safety, security, or prosperity, for they are now threats to them. We must turn toward true liberty, freedom, and private property given by our Creator, Who owns it all and bestows it upon us to have dominion over it under His authority.

Our next chapter delves into the eugenic inclinations of John Maynard Keynes, which would ultimately be the foundation of his phrase, the "Euthanasia of the Rentier."

THE ECONOMICS OF EUGENICS

EUGENICS

"The study of how to arrange reproduction within a human population
to increase heritable characteristics is regarded as desirable. Primarily
developed by Francis Galton to improve the human race, it fell into
disfavor only after the perversion of its doctrines by the Nazis."

"The most important, significant, and I would add, genuine
branch of sociology which exists, namely eugenics."
John Maynard Keynes—February 14, 1946

THIS CHAPTER DETAILS the little-known fact that John Maynard Keynes was an advocate of eugenics. As discussed in our previous chapters, worldview matters, and Keynes demonstrates the dark corridors of his mind and how they influenced his thinking. Before we begin, we must look at who influenced Keynes's thinking on this particular subject regarding population control through eugenics.

Thomas Malthus (1766-1834) was a British Economist who wrote, in 1798, the book called *An Essay on the Principle of Population*. Malthus wrote the following:

"Yet in all societies, even those that are most vicious, the tendency to a virtuous attachment [i.e., marriage] is so strong that there is a constant effort towards an increase of population. This constant effort as constantly tends to subject the lower classes of the society to distress and to prevent any great permanent amelioration of their condition."

In addition to Keynes studying the works of Malthus, he was also an avid student of heredity and genetics. Keynes was dubbed by his students Jeremiah Malthus. It is easy to see how Keynes embarked on his understanding of population growth. To manage this growth, a given population needed an eye toward maintaining a "desirable" racial stock. As Keynes's views of his economic theories expanded, his underlying beliefs about eugenics remained solidly intact. Keynes was a member of the British Eugenics Society, whereas, in 1946, he had served as its Vice President for seven years. Below is a sampling of his thoughts that reveal his eugenics ideas and how they shaped his economic theories.

New Republic Magazine—1923

"Is NOT A COUNTRY overpopulated when its standards are lower than they would be if its numbers were less? In that case, the question of what numbers are desirable rises long before starvation sets in, and even before, the level of life begins to fall. Perhaps we have already sacrificed too much for the population. For is not the improvement in the average conditions of life during the past century very small in comparison with the extraordinary material progress of that period? Does it not seem that the greater part of man's achievements are already swallowed up in the support of mere numbers? It is easy to understand the distaste provoked by particular methods, and the fear inspired by any proposal to modify the laissez-faire of nature and to bring the workings of a fundamental instinct under social control. But it is strange to be untroubled or to deny the existence of the problem for our generation."

Keynes's Lecture as recorded in 1925 by Margaret Sanger at the Conference on Population in Geneva:

"I AM DISCOURAGED because they are not striking at fundamentals. They do not want to think of one fundamental question, and that is the population question. There is not a city, not a country, in the League of Nations today that will accept it, or discuss it, and until the nations of the world are willing to sit down and talk about their problems from the population point of view, its rate of growth, its distribution, and its quality, they might just as well throw their peace proposals into the wastebasket, because they will never have international peace until they do consider that problem."

University of Berlin Lecture—June 23, 1926

"THE TIME HAS already come when each country needs a considered national policy about what size population, whether larger or smaller than at present or the same, is the most expedient. And having settled this policy, we must take steps to carry it into operation. The time may arrive a little later when the community as a whole must pay attention to the innate quality as well as to the mere numbers of its future members."

These ideas and others like them were the underpinnings of Hitler's Final Solution on the Jewish population of Nazi Germany. Further, Murray Rothbard, in his book *Keynes the Man*, discusses the German Edition of Keynes's book *The General Theory*, which had a unique introduction that says the following:

"Nevertheless, the theory of output as a whole, which is what the following book purports to provide, is **much more easily adapted to the conditions of a totalitarian state**, than is the theory of production and distribution of a given output produced under conditions of free competition and a lance measure of laissez-faire."

By John Maynard Keynes's admission, his thinking is more aligned with totalitarianism, complete with State-sponsored population control.

Keynes's Malthusian League Dinner Speech—1927

"I BELIEVE THAT for the future the problem of population will emerge in the much greater problem of heredity and eugenics. Mankind has taken into his own hands and out of the hands of nature, the task and the duty of molding history and his soul to a pattern."

Economic Possibilities for Our Grandchildren is one of the best-known writings of John Maynard Keynes. This book began as a lecture for school children in 1928. In this book, Keynes outlines what he would deem "our destination of economic bliss." To achieve "Economic Bliss," Keynes lays out the following considerations:

"Our power to control populations, our determination to avoid wars and civil dissensions, our willingness to entrust science the direction of these matters which are properly the concern of science, and the rate of accumulation as fixed by the margin between our production and our consumption; of which the last will easily look after itself, given the first three."

Because of his self-professed neo-Malthusian views, his economics were tools of central planning complete with population control. Keynes, the Social Darwinist and Technocrat of his day, feared a situation where "lower class" births would outpace the genetically fit and, by doing so, reduce the average quality of society and, consequently, the average level of prosperity.

As a continuation of his work called *The General Theory*, it is consistent with the idea of "population equilibrium" as a pre-condition for success. Also, the issue of unemployment and a host of other economic ills could be cured with this perceived "population equilibrium."

Interestingly enough, John Maynard Keynes had a hatred for the Puritan notion of thrift. Keynes despised and sought to remove this thrift as the ignition and engine of investment and production that would ultimately sustain a growing population free of any centralized government controls. Keynes's disdain for thrift blinded him to its merits. His Malthusian deceptions of population control reinforced Hitler's and Margaret Sanger's bigoted egocentricities and countless others who have left a wake of collateral damage in their path. All from the worldview of one man who rose to prominence in the world of economics.

Fast forward to today's world, and we see the Malthusian worldview once again. Modern-Day Social Darwinist Technocrats are ushering in their eugenicist plans of mandatory vaccines and vaccine passports while working hand in hand with the centralized planners of a totalitarian government, all in the name of one thing—population control.

THE EUTHANASIA OF THE RENTIER

"Go to the ant, O sluggard; consider her ways, and be wise.
Without having any chief, officer, or ruler, she prepares her
bread in summer and gathers her food in harvest."
Proverbs 6:6-8 (ESV)

"We must so use and possess the goods we have for (1) the glory of God, (2)
the salvation of our souls, (3) the maintenance of our good estates, (4) the
good of our family or kindred, (5) the relief of the poor, (6) the maintenance
of the Church, and (7) the maintenance of the Commonwealth."
William Perkins (1558-1602)—Puritan

"It will be, moreover, a great advantage of the order of events which I am
advocating, that the Euthanasia of the Rentier, of the functionless investor,
will be nothing sudden, merely a gradual but prolonged continuance of what
we have seen recently, in Great Britain, and will need no revolution."
John Maynard Keynes—General Theory (1936)

IN LIGHT OF what is happening with our current interest rate environment and its damaging impact on savers, we reveal to our readers *the euthanasia of the rentier*. The term coined by John Maynard Keynes is a pleasant way of saying the painless killing of the middle class through interest rate manipulation. Once again, these economic ideas come from a worldview promulgated by a deep-seated hatred for Puritan virtues. To further understand Keynes's desired euthanasia, we must first understand his motivations. The best source for this understanding comes from Murray Rothbard's book *Keynes the Man*. In it, Murray Rothbard states the following: "In *General Theory*, Keynes set forth a unique politico-economic sociology, dividing the population of each country into several rigidly separated economic classes, each with its own implicit moral evaluation. First, there is the mass of consumers; dumb, robotic, their behavior fixed and totally determined by external forces. In Keynes's assertion, the main force is a rigid proportion to their income, namely, their determined 'consumption function.' Second, there is a subset of consumers, an **eternal problem for mankind**: the insufferably bourgeois (middle class) savers, those who practice the solid Puritan values of thrift and farsightedness, those whom Keynes, the would-be aristocrat, **despised all his life**. All previous economists, certainly including Keynes's forbears Smith, Ricardo, and Marshall, had all lauded thrifty savers as building up long-term capital and, therefore, as responsible for enormous long-term improvements in consumers' standard of living. But, in a feat of prestidigitation (magic tricks performed as entertainment), severed the evident link between savings and investment, claiming instead the two are unrelated."

Essentially, the Rentier is a person who will put their savings into a bank, acting as a creditor to that bank. From here, the bank can lend, and in many cases, that lending could be to businesses to expand capital and production. This Rentier, in exchange, receives interest on their savings completing the transaction. The saver is contributing the seed corn to the economic system. In the upside-down world of John Maynard Keynes, this individual needed to be euthanized to make way for a very different kind of creditor. Because John Maynard Keynes was a Socialist, he sought to create economic policies based on government controls and central banking.

Murray Rothbard continues in his book. "By also severing interest returns from the price of time or from the real economy and by making it only a monetary phenomenon, Keynes was able to advocate, as a linchpin of his basic program, the 'Euthanasia of the Rentier' class: that is, the State's expanding the quantity of money enough so as to drive down the **rate of interest to zero**, thereby, at last, wiping out the **hated** creditors."

It should be noted that savings are seen as a virtue that protects us from economic shock and makes individuals and countries resilient to those shocks. Saving is delayed gratification and can also be seen as a delayed expenditure. These savings are used to manage future expenses, especially those that come in the golden years of retirement. On the contrary, a manipulated interest rate environment, especially with interest rates near zero or in some cases negative like in Europe, instead of saving and accumulating resources for the future, the society now relies on the government and the central banks to provide endless supplies of printed money. Sadly, this printed money comes in the form of debt. Instead of saving and delayed gratification, we find ourselves turned into the mass consumers that Keynes defined as performing our consumption function. We are now the dumb, robotic pawns of a never-ending spiral of debt that traps us in a state of perpetual bondage.

We now see a chain reaction unfold because the Rentier has been euthanized, and the seed corn of capital and production has already been eaten. As we now see in the Payroll Protection Program (PPP), broke companies need bailouts; unemployed workers cannot pay their rents, mortgages, or credit cards. Banks find themselves on the brink of loan defaults and foreclosures potentially requiring bailouts akin to 2008, and the mass of consumers find themselves living paycheck to paycheck or on unemployment merely trying to survive.

Our government is promising bailout after bailout during our current economic crisis due to Covid-19. Does the question now become how are these debts going to be paid off? The only mechanism now left is future taxation. However, our government has already spent our future taxation to pay the interest on our existing debt and continues to issue more and more bonds to acquire more and more debt. Yet, with the Rentier euthanized, who has any savings to purchase those bonds?

Today's Rentiers are our retirees supplementing their social security income and possibly pension payments through interest earnings on savings. This interest earned, in many cases, is allocated toward spending in a consumptive manner that keeps the economy moving along. However, these retirees struggle to make ends meet with zero interest rates, which siphons money out of the economy. Essentially, this is the confiscation of private property due to zero interest rates and the ongoing inflation that diminishes the purchasing power of these savings.

Contrary to Keynes's claims, this is not the painless killing of the middle class. It is the wholesale destruction of the engine of our economy that now threatens to imperil our future and our global civilization. We are now indentured servants to the government and the central bank, which opens the door to more control and more monetary manipulations. The question becomes, how long will the masses have confidence in the governments around the world until there is no one left to purchase their bonds, leading to the collapse of sovereign debt. Will our generation witness the failure of Keynesianism along with all the Elites whose power is tied to it?

It should be evident that worldview does matter. More importantly, a worldview removed from the Word of God leads to ideologies and theories that are in direct opposition to God due to man's sinful nature. We can see that John Maynard Keynes had a loathsome disdain for the Puritans, who were the forerunners of Christian Principles. Only a professed immoralist could devise an economic theory to euthanize these Puritan virtues, which he despised. Only the Truth can set us free. Long live the Rentier!

THOMAS PIKETTY
"CAPITAL IN THE 21ST CENTURY"

"You shall not move your neighbor's landmark, which the
men of old have set, in the inheritance that you will hold in
the land that the Lord your God is giving you to possess."

Deuteronomy 19:14

THIS CHAPTER DELVES into the dangerous rise of neo-Marxist economics. Thomas Piketty is a French economist who wrote the book
Capital in the 21st Century, published by Harvard. Piketty is a Professor
of Economics at the School for Advanced Studies in the Social Sciences
(EHESS), Associate Chair at the Paris School of Economics, and Cen-
tennial Professor of Economics in the International Inequalities Institute
at the London School of Economics. John Maynard Keynes and Karl
Marx have influenced his work. His mentor was Anthony Atkinson, who
Piketty called "the godfather of historical studies of income and wealth."
This dynamic duo of inequality put together a database on top incomes.

Thomas Piketty's book is a modern-day roadmap for the aspiring
Marxists amongst us who scream from the rooftops about rising inequality
as the result of rampant capitalism run amok. This book influences economics, governments, and universities in America and is the new coffee
table book of the left. Even more impressive is how Mr. Piketty focuses
on three nations' rising income inequality: the United States, the United
Kingdom, and Canada. Piketty's 685-page book reflects Karl Marx's book
called *Capital*. Piketty advocates an 80 percent tax on those earning over
$500,000 per year and an additional wealth tax.

What is even more disturbing is how Piketty has in his mind a capitalistic apocalypse whereby a contingent of elites will purchase everything and everybody, including the governments around the world. Therefore, he is advocating a complete overthrow of capitalism. In the *National Review*, James Pethokoukis said Mr. Piketty's "economic agenda is successfully pushed by Washington Democrats and by the mainstream media." Also, he writes, "The soft Marxism in *Capital in the 21st Century*, if unchallenged, will spread among the clerisy and reshape the political-economic landscape on which all future policy battles will be waged. Who will make the intellectual case for economic freedom today."

In addition, the Wall Street Journal's Daniel Shuchman calls Piketty's book "less a work of economic analysis than a bizarre ideological creed." Further, Shuchman writes that "Mr. Piketty assumes that the economy is a static and zero-sum; if the income of one population group increases, another must necessarily have been impoverished. He views equality of outcome as the ultimate end and solely for its own sake."

Now we turn to a quote from Thomas Piketty's book Capital in the 21st Century, where he writes the following: "To be sure, there exists in principle a quite simple economic mechanism that should restore equilibrium to the process: the mechanism of supply and demand. If the supply of any good is insufficient and its price is too high, then demand for that good should decrease, which should lead to a decline in its price. In other words, if real estate and oil prices rise, then people should move to the country or take to traveling about by bicycle (or both). Never mind that such adjustments might be unpleasant or complicated; they might also take decades, during which landlords and oil well owners might well accumulate claims on the rest of the population so extensive that they could easily come to own everything that can be owned, including rural real estate and bicycles, once and for all."

The lack of economic rigor, especially regarding all the rural real estate and bicycles being owned once and for all, is quite stunning. In the stroke of a pen, Piketty moves from the free market principle of supply and demand, which then morphs into no one owning a bicycle over a period of time. Piketty seems to ignore that owning everything, including an unlimited wealth concentration, is impossible in a free market economy. Piketty, in his book, seems to ignore the role of entrepreneurialism, the laws of competitive advantage, and the division of labor. Also discounted is the consumer's part, leading to the invisible hand of commerce and the principle of supply and demand. The market will make the necessary adjustments, and by doing so, the ownership of bicycles and land will be preserved for the population. In Piketty's mind, the only solution to the problem he sees with capitalism run amok is destroying wealth through onerous taxation on a global scale. Also, Piketty is opposed to inheritances and retirement funds because those assets are not shared with the collective.

In Thomas Piketty, we see an idyllic egalitarian seeking to be a neo-Platonian philosopher-king taking from the rich and giving to the poor in a global redistribution of wealth scheme. Perhaps this is why his book is the roadmap for Marxist operatives. The nineteenth century British economist David Ricardo coined a phrase called Rent-Seeking. In public-choice theory and economics, rent-seeking means seeking to increase one's share of existing wealth without creating new wealth. Rent-seeking results in reduced economic efficiency through misallocation of resources, reduced wealth creation, lost government revenue, **heightened income inequality**, and **potential national decline**. Rent-seeking is an attempt to obtain economic rent (i.e., the portion of income paid to a factor of production more than what is needed to keep it employed in its current use) by manipulating the social or political environment in which economic activities occur, rather than by creating new wealth. **Rent-seeking implies the extraction of uncompensated value from others without making any contribution to productivity.** Rent-seeking is distinguished in theory from profit-seeking, in which entities seek to extract value by engaging in mutually beneficial transactions. Profit-seeking, in this sense, is the creation of wealth. At the same time, **rent-seeking is "profiteering" by using social institutions, such as the power of the state, to redistribute wealth among different groups without creating** new wealth. An example of rent-seeking involves lobbying groups on behalf of corporations to obtain grants, subsidies, or tariff protection from the government. These protect or benefit the corporations with no additional wealth being created for society.

Rent-seeking is nothing new and has existed since time began. It transfers wealth from one person to another and uses big government and all the associated corruption to achieve its goal. The very idea of rent-seeking is handing over the reins of wealth redistribution to a few, which worsens income inequality. The solution is the problem that leads to a downward spiral of economic devastation. We would now like to turn our attention toward The Heidelberg Catechism, adopted in 1563 by a synod in Heidelberg. We find a question pertaining to the violation of the eighth commandment from the Bible. In question 110 of the Heidelberg Catechism, it asks what does God forbid in the eighth commandment. The answer is as follows: "Not only such theft and robbery as are punished by the magistrate; but God views as theft **all wicked tricks and devices, whereby we seek to draw to ourselves our neighbor's goods, whether by force or with show of right, such as unjust weights, measures, wares, coins, usury, or any means forbidden of God; so moreover all covetousness, and all useless waste of His gifts.**"

Redistribution of wealth is the epitome of covetousness by those who promote rent-seeking, all under the guise of income inequality. Income inequality is simply another wicked trick and device of Communism, which has been tried forty-two times in the last 100 years. It has failed in unimaginable ways, leading to the loss of lives resulting from disease, starvation, and violence. The only remedy for income inequality is for the free markets to operate in their purest form, and by doing so, all of society is elevated. The ownership of private property, which facilitates wealth creation free from government intervention, leads to productivity and, more importantly, job creation.

Although capitalism has its flaws, we must remember that those flaws come from man's fallen nature. When man calibrates his mind to God's Word and submits himself to the authority of God, our economic system flourishes, letting us learn the value of stewardship and the great opportunity God gives us to demonstrate generosity and giving. It is the changed heart of man that gradually and over time diminishes income inequality, not a rent-seeking state filled with corruption and self-serving covetousness.

Our next chapter will delve into the mind and depraved Nimrodian ideology of Klaus Schwab, who many consider a threat to our global civilization.

WHO IS KLAUS SCHWAB?

*"For what will it profit a man if he gains the
whole world, and loses his own soul?"*
Mark 8:36 (NKJV)

W E NOW TURN our attention to a discussion about Klaus Schwab,
who many consider to be the world's most dangerous man. Before
we begin, it is essential to note that an individual is not born with a worldview. Our worldview is shaped by many factors that ultimately form
our identity. The factors which shape our worldview over time include
family, friends, community, education, cultural and societal peer pressures, and the life circumstances and historical events that we have lived.
Many of us can tell stories about how our grandparents went through
the depression and World War II. These events greatly impacted their
lives as well as their worldview.

We want to take our readers back to the year 1938 in Nazi Germany
for this chapter. This year saw a Fascist Dictator named Adolf Hitler rise
to power. This year saw the following events unfold. Hitler abolished the
war ministry, which gave him direct control over the German military.
German troops occupied Austria, followed by the annexation of Austria
by Germany. There was the invasion of Czechoslovakia, the expulsion
of 12,000 Polish Jews living in Germany, 17,000 Polish Jews deported
to Poland, and the beginning of the Holocaust on November 9th with
Kristallnacht, also known as the night of broken glass. The all-night affair
saw Nazi activists loot and burn businesses resulting in 7,500 Jewish
businesses being destroyed, 267 Synagogues burned, ninety-one Jews
killed, and at least 25,000 Jewish men arrested. The year 1938 was the

spark that lit the raging fires of World War II. This era is considered to be one of the most horrific periods of the twentieth century. This singular point in time scarred the lives and worldview of many who were part of this historical moment.

It is essential to understand this period because Klaus Schwab was born on March 30, 1938, in Ravensburg, Germany. Very little is known about his childhood. The only available information is that his father was a businessman who went over the border to Switzerland, leaving him and his mother alone in war-torn Germany. There have been speculations that Klaus Schwab's father was indeed a Nazi operative. A young Klaus Schwab grew up and was influenced by these events, especially the notion of borders, destruction, and death. On the other end of the spectrum were Adolf Hitler's diabolical ambitions to take over the world, ushering in the Third Reich that would reign for one thousand years. As Klaus Schwab grew, he lived in a country that used a police state built on fear and violence, brown shirts and operatives, surveillance, brainwashing and control, propaganda and lies, the merger of government and businesses, eugenics, dehumanization, and a focus on hygiene. Today Klaus Schwab heads up the World Economic Forum and is the Great Reset's driving force. Our next chapter will delve into the Great Reset or, more aptly stated, the Fascist assault of the twenty-first century. For this chapter, we need to explore Klaus Schwab's mind and see if we can draw parallels in his thinking to the events that shaped his life in Nazi Germany.

Klaus Schwab wrote many books, including his latest book published in 2020 called *Covid-19: The Great Reset*. We would now like to delve into some of his thinking, which spans many years of his career. To begin, Mr. Schwab seems to be fascinated with transhumanism, where he sees a merger of humans and machines which in his own words, will be "curious mixes of digital and analog life." He delights in "sensors, memory switches and circuits that can be encoded in common human gut bacteria" and that "Smart Dust, arrays of full computers with antennas, each much smaller than a grain of sand, can now organize themselves inside the body" and that "implanted devices will likely also help to communicate thoughts normally expressed verbally through a built-in smartphone, and potentially unexpressed thoughts or mood by reading brain waves and other signals." With these ideas, one cannot help but think of Josef Mengele, also known as the Angel of Death, who conducted medical experiments on the Jews in concentration camps.

Also, Mr. Schwab gleefully states, "That it is now far easier to manipulate with precision the human genome within viable embryos means that we are likely to see the advent of **designer babies** in the future who possess **particular traits** or who are **resistant to specific diseases**." Adolf Hitler would be proud of Klaus Schwab's quest for a Master Race of people. As if this is not alarming enough, Schwab is now using the pandemic to promote his personal version of hygiene. According to Klaus Schwab, "The pandemic will certainly heighten our focus on hygiene. A new obsession with cleanliness will particularly entail the creation of new forms of packaging. We will be encouraged not to touch the products we buy. Simple pleasures like smelling a melon or squeezing a fruit will be frowned upon and may even become a thing of the past." To many, this may seem like the mental meanderings of an eighty-three-year-old man with early-onset dementia. However, we would be remiss if we did not refer to what Susan Bachrach, Ph.D., wrote in the *New England Journal of Medicine* on July 29th, 2004: "In democratic societies, the needs of public health sometimes require citizens to make sacrifices for the greater good, but in Nazi Germany, national or public health—Volksgesundheit—took complete precedence over individual health care. Physicians and medically trained academics, many of whom were proponents of 'racial hygiene,' or eugenics, legitimized and helped to implement Nazi policies aiming to 'cleanse' the German Society of people viewed as biologic threats to the nation's health. Racial-hygiene measures began with the mass sterilization of the 'genetically diseased' and ended with the near-annihilation of European Jewry." Further Schwab states as it pertains to the Covid-19 pandemic that "the next hurdle is the political challenge of vaccinating enough people worldwide (we are collectively as strong as the weakest link) with a high enough compliance rate despite the rise of anti-vaxxers." The question here becomes who comprises the weakest link, which is perhaps a veiled statement about the German idea of "racial hygiene" or eugenics.

Growing up in a Fascist state, Schwab writes the following in his book *Covid-19: The Great Reset*, "One of the greatest lessons of the past five centuries in Europe and America is this: acute crises contribute to boosting the state's power. It's always been the case, and there is no reason why it should be different with the Covid-19 pandemic." And what better way to do that than with youth activism. According to Schwab, "Youth activism is increasing worldwide, being revolutionized by social media that increases mobilization to an extent that would have been impossible before it. It takes many different forms, ranging from non-institutionalized political participation to demonstrations and protests, and addresses issues as diverse as climate change, economic reforms, gender equality, and LGBTQ rights. The young generation is firmly at the vanguard of social change. There is little doubt that it will be the catalyst for change and a source of critical momentum for the Great Reset." Here we see digital brown shirts mobilized using social media, another mechanism of lies and propaganda to usher in Klaus Schwab's agenda.

As we can see, Schwab has been impacted by his childhood growing up under a totalitarian Fascist State. Growing up in Fascist Germany, this significant event has influenced his worldview, as seen from his writings. Perhaps the young Klaus admired Hitler's ambitions for world domination since Schwab's organization, the World Economic Forum, has global governance ambitions. Hitler was convinced that his Third Reich would last for a thousand years. Instead, it came crashing down, destroying Germany while Adolf Hitler committed suicide. With all its influential members, Klaus Schwab's World Economic Forum is our modern-day Fourth Reich. Like the one before it, this too shall fail, but we will experience maladjustments to the global economy on its way to failure.

As believers, we must hold fast to the Word of God. We must heed the words of 1 Peter 1:13 (NKJV), "Therefore gird up the loins of your mind, be sober, and rest your hope fully upon the grace that is to be brought to you at the revelation of Jesus Christ." It is time for every Christian to fasten our seat belts, roll up our sleeves, and prepare our minds for the coming spiritual exertion that is coming upon us. Our next chapter lays out what Klaus Schwab's Great Reset plan means to the world.

Praise the Lord, all nations! Extol him, all people!
For great is his steadfast love toward us, and the faithfulness
of the Lord endures forever. Praise the Lord!

Psalm 117

THE GREAT FASCIST RESET

*"For as the heavens are higher than the
earth, so are my ways higher than your ways
and my thoughts than your thoughts."*
Isaiah 55:9

*"The pandemic gives us this chance: it represents
a rare but narrow window of opportunity to
reflect, reimagine and reset our world."*
Klaus Schwab—*Covid-19: The Great Reset*

IN OUR LAST chapter, we peered into the mind of Klaus Schwab, head
of the World Economic Forum. We established that Schwab sees the
world through his experiences living in Nazi Germany. This experience
has influenced his worldview. Schwab established the World Economic
Forum on January 24, 1971. This organization acts as a non-governmental
and lobbying organization. Approximately 1,000 member companies
fund it. The World Economic Forum hosts its annual meeting in Davos,
Switzerland. This organization has come under criticism, especially for
its involvement in a "global redesign" in partnership with the United
Nations. The Dutch Transnational Institute think tank has determined
that the Davos meetings are a silent coup d'état to capture governance.
We want to overview the critical points involving what Schwab calls the
Great Reset. Before we begin, we would like to quote Klaus Schwab and
his coauthor Thierry Malleret from their book *Covid-19: The Great Reset*.
These quotes should allow us to connect the dots regarding the Covid-

19 virus's real agenda. These authors admit that Covid-19 is "one of the **least** deadly pandemics in the last 2000 years." Also, "the consequences of the virus will be **mild** compared to previous pandemics." And lastly, Covid-19 "does **not** constitute an existential threat or a shock that will leave its imprint on the world's population for decades." Yet, in their book *Covid-19: The Great Reset*, they state that "the pandemic gives us this chance: it represents a rare but narrow window of opportunity to reflect, reimagine and reset our world." Therefore, the lockdowns that have created economic disaster are designed to make a Great Reset of the world at large. Now we look at the broad objectives that the World Economic Forum and their influential partners seek to usher into our world by taking advantage of a virus that, per their words, is the least deadly with no long-term existential threat to our society.

The following is a list of their objectives based on a video from the World Economic Forum website. We will briefly comment on some of these objectives. We will find that this is a form of global Communist-Fascism underway.

1. You will own nothing and be happy about it.

As WE LEARNED in previous chapters, one of the first tenets of Communism is to abolish private property. Only this time, Mr. Schwab and his partners in crime seek to do this on a global scale. The lockdowns created massive economic imbalances that will only lead to the redistribution of wealth through onerous forms of taxation. Another concern discussed amongst economists is the overall debt structure amongst sovereign nations. Many fear that other lockdowns will continue to destabilize the global economic system, leading to debt cancellation. Many will undoubtedly cheer on having their debt canceled, which would include mortgages, car loans, and credit card debt. However, in exchange for that cancellation of debt, you would no longer have ownership of your home, car, or any other asset for which debt is attached. According to Klaus Schwab, the Covid-19 virus is not a significant threat; however, the measures to deal with it are draconian at best, leading us to believe that the ulterior motive behind the virus is the Great Reset.

2. Whatever you want, you will rent it, and it will be delivered to you by drone.

SINCE THERE WILL be no private property ownership, you will rent what you want, and it will be delivered to you by drone. Does the question now become, what exactly are we renting? Are we renting our homes, cars, furniture, smartphones, and computers? Also, how are these rents being paid for? Here is where the concept of universal basic income comes into play. This is why there are constant clarion calls for "minimum wage." A minimum wage is a form of universal basic income. As of this writing, we see labor shortages in this country and other countries worldwide. Instead of legislating minimum wage, labor shortages are now creating increased wages. In Schwab's book *Covid-19: The Great Reset*, he writes, "Consumers need products and, if they can't shop, they will inevitably resort to purchasing them online. As the habit kicks in, people who had never shopped online before will become comfortable with doing so, while people who were part-time online shoppers before will presumably rely on it more. This was made evident during the lockdowns. In the United States, Amazon and Walmart hired a combined 250,000 workers to keep up with the increase in demand and built massive infrastructure to deliver online. This accelerating growth of e-commerce means that the giants of the online retail industry are likely to emerge from the crisis even stronger than they were in the pre-pandemic era." Here we see massive consolidation of power. As more and more workers get displaced in other industries, they may have no choice but to work at set wages for the big online retailers in warehouses or as part of the ever-expanding infrastructure, especially since, according to Schwab, we will be renting what we use. This is nothing less than neo-feudalism, whereby the technocratic elites own all aspects of production while allowing the peasants to serve them through labor and rented consumption.

3. The United States will not be the world's leading superpower.

THE UNITED STATES has something critical that lies at its foundation. It is called the Constitution. The Constitution acts as the lynchpin for America and the world at large. Remove this lynchpin, and we see a Totalitarian Technocracy rising up with a foundation built on Communism, Fascism, and Neo-Feudalism all rolled into one Authoritarian regime of World Domination. Klaus Schwab, in his book, says the following "Most people, fearful of the danger posed by Covid-19, will ask: Isn't it foolish not to leverage the power of technology to come to our rescue when we are victims of an outbreak and facing a life or death kind of situation? They will then be willing to give up a lot of privacy and will agree that in such circumstances, public power can rightfully override individual rights." These individual rights are preserved in the Constitution of the United States of America. These are the individual rights that God has bestowed upon us. Again, the objective is to remove the barrier of individual liberties and freedoms. Therefore, this is why the United States is explicitly being targeted with a virus that, according to Schwab, is not that deadly and poses no existential threat to society. The virus that does pose an existential threat is called Communism, which has now mutated into one of its most toxic forms.

4. A handful of countries will dominate.

THE QUESTION TO this statement becomes what countries will dominate. Could it be that the economic power will shift to China? China's form of Communism fits very well into the construct of what the World Economic Forum proposes, complete with social credit scores, social engineering, surveillance, and being cut off from society and locked up in prison for dissenting against the State. In his book, Schwab laments that "The more nationalism and isolationism pervade the global polity, the greater the chance that global governance loses its relevance and becomes ineffective. Sadly, we are now at this critical juncture. Put blatantly, we live in a world in which nobody is really in charge." He also writes, "Therefore, the concern is that, without appropriate global governance, we will become paralyzed in our attempts to address and respond to global challenges, particularly when there is such a strong dissonance between short-term domestic imperatives and long-term, global challenges. This is a major worry that today there is no 'committee to save the world.'" A committee to save the world is a euphemism for Global Totalitarianism. It will comprise a committee of the World Economic Forum and their influential partners from Big Tech, Big Pharma, the Corporate Food Industry, and the United Nations.

5. You will not die waiting for an organ donor. We will not transplant organs. We will print new ones instead.

WE ASK A SIMPLE question regarding this statement. Suppose actual organ transplants create a situation in the body where the transplanted organ will eventually lead to rejection, leading to death. Would the same not hold true for a printed organ? What should concern everyone is how the World Economic Forum is now intervening in healthcare. Their website concludes the following "Our current capital intensive, hospital-centric model is unsustainable and ineffective. The Platform for Shaping the Future of Health and Healthcare leverages data-enabled delivery systems and virtual care, integrated across the continuum of care from precision prevention to personal care delivery." Of course, aiding these incentives are Bill Gates, AstraZeneca, Bayer, Johnson & Johnson, Merck, Pfizer, Novartis, and a host of others. Printed organs and virtual care translate to the wholesale destruction of our healthcare system and the displacement of well-trained doctors, leading to a death sentence of individuals who need hands-on healthcare. Welcome to Medicare for All and Death Panels.

6. You will eat much less meat, an occasional treat, not a staple for the good of the environment and our health.

THIS IS NOTHING less than the Great Reset plan for our food industry. A November 9, 2020, article in The Defender, a new media platform by the Children's Health Defense, points out the problem with the World Economic Forum's involvement in the food industry. It states, "The architects of the plan claim it will reduce food scarcity, hunger, and disease, and even mitigate climate change. But a close look at the corporations and think tanks the World Economic Forum is partnering with to usher in this global transformation suggests that the real motive is tighter corporate control over the food system by means of technological solutions." To make matters worse, we have something called the EAT Forum and what can only be construed as the Rise of Food Imperialism. The EAT Forum was cofounded by the Wellcome Trust with the financial help of GlaxoSmithKline. According to The Defender, the ultimate aim of this organization is to "replace wholesome, nutritious food with genetically modified lab creations." Perhaps this is why we will need to transplant our organs with printed ones. The body was never designed to digest any form of lab-created foods, which will lead to a massive healthcare problem resulting from eating toxic chemicals. The "Planetary Health Diet" developed by EAT is a diet that is supposed to replace all others. Federic Leroy, a food science and biotechnology professor at the University of Brussels, told The Defender: "The diet aims to cut meat and dairy intake of the global population by as much as 90 percent in some cases and replaces it with lab-made foods, cereals, and oil." This is simply nothing less than a corporate takeover of the food system. Perhaps this is why Bill Gates and Jeff Bezos of Amazon are buying up farmland around the world. We would be remiss if we did not remind our readers how Socialism and starvation go hand in hand.

7. A billion people will be displaced by climate change. We will have to do a better job at welcoming and integrating refugees.

ONE OF THE tenets of Communism involves the gradual abolition of all distinctions between town and country by a more equitable distribution of the population over the country. In this case, we are not talking about a countrywide situation but a global situation. The catalyst for this event has to do with climate change. To think a billion people will be displaced is quite alarming. Perhaps this very situation will be caused by the same people instigating remedies for climate change that will lead to the exact displacement they are referring to. One of Klaus Schwab's favorite pastimes is geoengineering. It is Schwab who has said the following as it pertains to climate change: "Proposals include installing giant mirrors in the stratosphere to deflect the sun's rays, chemically seeding the atmosphere to increase rainfall and the deployment of large machines to remove carbon dioxide from the air." One finds themselves in a science fiction horror movie whereby we see a nuclear winter, mass flooding, crop failures, and carbon dioxide machines releasing toxic gases into the atmosphere leading to the displacement of a billion people. Only the return of Jesus Christ Himself can stop the carnage and save us all from these people.

8. Polluters will have to pay to emit carbon dioxide. There will be a global price on carbon. This will help make fossil fuels history.

IT IS INTERESTING to note that Klaus Schwab, in his book *Covid-19: The Great Reset* speaks of what he calls the Environmental Reset. He said the following: "Furthermore, in global risk terms, it is with climate change and ecosystem collapse (the two key environmental risks) that the pandemic most easily equates. The three represent, by nature and to varying degrees, existential threats to humankind, and we could argue that Covid-19 has already given us a glimpse, or foretaste, of what a full-fledged climate crisis and ecosystem collapse could entail from an economic perspective: combined demand and supply shocks, and disruption to trade and supply chains ripple and knock-on effects that amplify risks." His book also discusses the lockdowns and carbon emissions, demonstrating that estimates state that carbon emissions were reduced by approximately 8 percent due to the lockdowns. It is now evident that the lockdowns were used as an experiment to push through a climate change agenda since, by Schwab's own admission, Covid-19 is not an existential threat. Yet, it was used to simulate an ecosystem collapse. In his book *Apocalypse Never*, Michael Shellenberger writes, "*Apocalypse Never* explores how and why so many of us came to see important but manageable environmental problems as the end of the world, and why the people who are the most apocalyptic about environmental problems tend to oppose the best and most obvious solutions to solving them." More and more research supports the fact that climate change is out of our hands and is mainly driven or even partially driven by solar cycles. The actual apocalypse involves the taxation of carbon dioxide, which puts upward pricing pressure on everything produced because fossil fuels and their usage are more pervasive than the average person realizes. Therefore, this is the Communist-Fascist way of controlling production from the bottom-up, further destabilizing the global economy.

9. You could be preparing to go to Mars. Scientists will have worked out how to keep you healthy in space—the start of a journey to find alien life.

WE WILL NOT be commenting on the prospect of going to Mars. This is an uninhabitable planet, and this can be regarded as a fantasy of futuristic thinking that has no basis in reality unless Mars is the concentration camp for those who are dissidents against the World Economic Forum, aka Masters of the Universe.

10. Western values will have been tested to the breaking point. Checks and balances that underpin our Democracies must not be forgotten.

PERHAPS THIS IS what Klaus Schwab desires that Western Values built on Christianity be not only tested to the breaking point but are entirely suppressed. This will lead to checks and balances being swept away under censorship, social credit scores, digital currencies, and surveillance. In a remarkable statement from Covid-19: The Great Reset is the following:

"Radical changes of such consequences are coming that some pundits have referred to a 'before coronavirus' (BC) and 'after coronavirus' (AC) era. We will continue to be surprised by both the rapidity and unexpected nature of these changes—as they conflate with each other, they will provoke second, third, fourth, and more order consequences, cascading effects, and unforeseen outcomes. In so doing, they will shape a 'new normal' radically different from the one we will be progressively leaving behind. Many of our beliefs and assumptions about what the world could or should look like will be shattered in the process." Before Christ (BC), the non-Jewish world was held captive by the chains of sin and spiritual destitution. After Christ (AC), the world was given salvation and deliverance from this sinful nature, with the chains being broken once and for all by Christ. Now all reference to Him is removed as we have propelled ourselves forward from a Before Coronavirus (BC) world to an After Coronavirus (AC) world. We are essentially back to a pagan world complete with tyrannical dictators presiding over the peasant classes harkening back to the days of Medieval Europe. It was Christianity that liberated Medieval Europe. It will once again be Christianity that will deliver us from the Medieval state of this modern-day neo-feudalism that we now find ourselves in.

Now we must turn to the words of Dietrich Bonhoeffer, who said, "Silence in the face of evil is itself evil: God will not hold us guiltless. Not to speak is to speak. Not to act is to act." We can no longer be silent amidst the Great Reset!

THE GREAT RESET
STAKEHOLDER CAPITALISM

*"Capitalism was the only system in history where wealth was
not acquired by looting, but by production, not by force, but
by trade, the only system that stood for man's right to his own
mind, to his work, to his life, to his happiness, to himself."*
Ayn Rand

IN THIS CHAPTER, we focus on something called *Stakeholder Capitalism*.
In 2021, Klaus Schwab of the World Economic Forum and his coauthor
Peter Vanham wrote the book called Stakeholder Capitalism. Schwab
informs us that the book's views are based on his personal life experiences
in the book's preface. He also asks the reader to understand his worldview,
which ultimately means the world, according to Klaus Schwab.

Before we begin, we must first define what Stakeholder Capitalism
means. According to Investopedia, Stakeholder Capitalism is a system
in which corporations are oriented to serve all their stakeholders' interests. Among the key stakeholders are customers, suppliers, employees,
shareholders, and **societies at large**, including local communities. In
this perversion of Capitalism, the property owners, also known as the
shareholders, are no more significant than society. When we see the terms
societies at large or local communities, it is a subversive way of saying the
collective or, as in Stakeholder Capitalism—Corporate Socialism, which
will lead to economic fascism and neo-feudalism. The economist Murray
Rothbard stated the following: "Whenever someone begins to talk about
'society' or 'society's interest coming before 'mere individuals and their

interests,' a good operative rule is: guard your pocketbook, and guard yourself! Because behind the façade of 'society,' there is always a group of power-hungry doctrinaires and exploiters, ready to take your money and to order your actions and your life. For somehow, they are society!" The economist Milton Friedman said, "Few trends could so thoroughly undermine the very foundations of our free society as the acceptance by corporate officials of a social responsibility other than to make as much money for their stockholders as possible. This is a fundamentally subversive doctrine. If businessmen do have a social responsibility other than making maximum profits for stockholders, how are they to know what it is? Can self-selected private individuals decide what the social interest is? Can they decide how great a burden they are justified in placing on themselves or their stockholders to serve that social interest?" Interestingly enough, Klaus Schwab is not a big fan of Milton Friedman.

In his book *Stakeholder Capitalism*, Klaus Schwab states the following: "The world currently knows two prevailing and competing economic systems: Shareholder Capitalism, which is dominant in the United States and in many other countries in the West, and State Capitalism, which is championed by China and is gaining popularity in many other emerging markets." Further, Mr. Schwab states: "But each has equally brought about major social, economic, and environmental downsides. They led to rising inequalities of income, wealth, and opportunity, increased tensions between the haves and have nots, and above all, a mass degradation of the environment. Given the shortcomings of both of these systems, we believe we need a new, better global system: Stakeholder Capitalism. In this system, the interests of all stakeholders in the economy and society are taken on board, companies optimize for more than just short-term profits, and **governments are the guardians** of equality of opportunity, a level-playing field in competition, and a fair contribution of and distribution to all stakeholders with regards to the sustainability and inclusivity of the system."

In these sentences, we can see that Schwab attempts to reconcile Capitalism and Communism/Socialism. There is a term for this, and it is called Interventionism. This is where governmental powers and organizations like the World Economic Forum think they have the right to intervene in the free market to suit their plans for society. It is important to note that those who advocate for Interventionism do it under the guise of lofty social goals, bringing about a utopian world that is good for all, only to see that utopia shattered into a million pieces by tyranny and totalitarianism. In today's modern world of economics, we are already dealing with government intervention through taxation and regulations as well as by special interest groups. This Interventionism causes the very problems they then seek to rectify. This current mutation of Stakeholder Capitalism will create further economic distortion and potentially destabilize the global economy far beyond what centralized socialist planning could do. In partnership with the World Economic Forum, the technocratic elites, governments, and international agencies could easily determine consumer needs and wants by limiting the production of goods and services as we already see with the war on fossil fuels in exchange for renewable energy. In essence, we are witnessing a global purging of both individual and private property rights through the use of a pandemic to create a neo-feudalist reset of the world. Ayn Rand said, "Individual rights are not subject to a public vote; a majority has no right to vote away the rights of a minority; the political function of rights is precisely to protect minorities from oppression by majorities (and the smallest minority on earth is the individual)."

Many may be wondering how such a feat of global economic intervention with all the hallmarks of Fascism, Marxism, and Feudalism rolled into one could be successful. The answer to this question is to utilize what is called being Woke. The definition of being Woke refers to a perceived awareness of issues that concern social justice and racial justice. Also, those who are Woke are part of what is being called the cancel culture. Cancel culture refers to the widespread practice of withdrawing support for (canceling) public figures and companies after they have done or said something considered objectionable or offensive. Cancel culture is generally discussed as being performed on social media in the form of group shaming. They are also tearing down our American society's established history and customs. This cancel culture is forcing corporate America to bow down to their demands, which could be called Woke Capitalism, which is Klaus Schwab's dream of Stakeholder Capitalism.

In many ways, being Woke is a perversion of Marxism. Marxism aimed to have the proletariat rise against the business class to strip away private property and redistribute wealth. The dominant class, in this case, was the worker class. The target of Marxism was the middle-class business owners and entrepreneurs who create employment. With Wokism, the dominant class is based on gender, race, and sexual orientation. What is potentially happening is a situation whereby the technocratic elites through the World Economic Forum are funding this movement of Wokism. It is designed to fragment and fracture the working class, which prevents unity and, as in any Marxist revolution, turns them against large corporations so they will embrace Stakeholder Capitalism. All now succumb to the Great Reset.

Once again, the goal is the full-on destruction of Capitalism. Milton Friedman said, "The great virtue of a free market system is that it does not care what color people are; it does not care what their religion is; it only cares whether they can produce something you want to buy. It is the most effective system we have discovered to enable people who hate one another to deal with one another and help one another." Capitalism and the free markets propel men and women to their highest potentials and, in the process, diminish inequality and elevate all to a higher standard of living. Ayn Rand said, "America's abundance was created not by public sacrifices to the common good, but by the productive genius of free men who pursued their own personal interests and the making of their own private fortunes. They did not starve the people to pay for America's industrialization. They gave the people better jobs, higher wages, and cheaper goods with every new machine they invented, with every scientific discovery or technological advance—and thus the whole country was moving forward and profiting, not suffering, every step of the way."

To make matters more alarming as to Stakeholder Capitalism's direction, we would like to share a recent development. Justin Danhof wrote in *The Federalist* the following: "Nasdaq seeks to coerce company boards to adhere to new 'diversity' quotas based on race, sex, and sexual behavior" and "Nasdaq's recent pronouncement that it plans to **delist any company** from its exchange that won't appoint board members based on how they look, whether they have sex with the 'right' people, or identify as a letter in the LGBT lexicon. Nasdaq's dictate is wholly unconstitutional, panders to minority groups and women, and would **financially strain many American businesses.** Still, it's pushing forward anyway because it thinks no one will have the courage to stand up and stop it. Specifically, Nasdaq is seeking permission from the U.S. Securities and Exchange Commission (SEC) to **delist any American company from its platform unless the company puts two 'diverse' individuals on its board of directors. One position must be given to a female. And one position must be given to a racial minority or a member of the ever-broadening definition of LGBT."**

The implications of this are truly staggering. If a particular company refuses to go along with this agenda, the Woke mob will be unleashed in a social media frenzy. This could cause irreparable damage to a company's reputation as it attempts to explain its stance on the matter. This could lead to the Woke mob's accusations that the company directors are racists, sexists, or homophobes. Worse, it could start potential boycotts or Nasdaq delisting the company, which would create problems for the shareholder value. This unleashes a spiral that could put the company out of business when it does not have access to capital due to being delisted from the exchange leading to bankruptcy and devastating job losses. Welcome to Klaus Schwab's vision of Stakeholder Capitalism.

The Great Reset has leveraged the Woke mob to do its bidding. The agenda is clear. As Christian conservatives, we must work together to combat this insidious situation we find ourselves in. There are ways for us to respond.

Instead of shopping online through companies like Amazon, support your local small businesses.

- Likewise, avoid big box stores and head for your local small business retailer.
- Consider starting a part-time home business. Self-employed people do not have to be worried about being fired over their political opinions.
- We also suggest forming networks with other Christian conservatives and doing business with them.
- We must also refuse to comply with their demands, especially if another forced lockdown is imposed on us.
- We also may want to explore setting up barter networks with fellow Christians and conservatives.
- Christians especially should maintain fellowship with one another and encourage small group meetings.
- Christian conservatives working in large companies can form groups within the workplace to address the dramatic changes pertaining to Woke capitalism.

There is indeed power in numbers, and we cannot succumb to the propaganda that implies newer and deadlier mutations of the Covid-19 virus. The true variant is global communism which is being ushered in by the Great Reset! This is the great mutation of Capitalism!

"Finally, be strong in the Lord and in the strength of his might. Put on the whole armor of God, that you may be able to stand against the schemes of the devil. For we do not wrestle against flesh and blood, but against the rulers, against the authorities, against the cosmic powers over this present darkness, against the spiritual forces of evil in the heavenly places."
Ephesians 6:10-12 (ESV)

"Ask yourself why totalitarian dictatorships find it necessary to pour money and effort into propaganda for their own helpless, chained, gagged slaves, who have no means of protest or defense. The answer is that even the humblest peasant or the lowest savage would rise in blind rebellion, were he to realize that he is being immolated, not to some incomprehensible noble purpose, but to plain, naked human evil."

Ayn Rand

THE BATTLE FOR OUR MINDS

"And in the midst of this wide quietness, a rosy sanctuary
will I dress, With the wreath'd trellis of a working brain."
John Keats, Ode to Psyche

"Do not be conformed to this world, but be transformed by the
renewal of your mind, that by testing you may discern what is
the will of God, what is good and acceptable and perfect."
Romans 12:2 (ESV)

MANY ARE NOW asking how did we get to this point? What is currently
happening to many in our society who seem to be in a state of mass
psychosis? As we have learned, there is now a consolidation of power
amongst the technocratic elites. To know the direction we are going in,
we must understand the impact of technology on our lives. Because in
many ways, we live in an Orwellian world, and many wonder how we
arrived here so quickly or so it seems on the surface. As a result of a virus
that we have learned poses no existential threat to society, we are now
confronting an array of totalitarian measures that have not been seen
since Nazi Germany. However, what we are facing is far worse because
of the influence of social media and other forms of propaganda and
censorship. As we can surmise, this has all been by design, and this war
is being waged on the battlefield of our minds.

In his book *Covid-19: The Great Reset*, Klaus Schwab writes, "The
most effective form of tracking or tracing is obviously one powered by
technology: it not only allows backtracking all the contacts with whom
the user of a mobile phone has been in touch but also tracking the user's

real-time movements, which in turn affords the possibility to better enforce a lockdown and to warn other mobile users in proximity of the carrier that they have been exposed to someone infected." This level of surveillance even pervades our working lives. We also read the following; "The corporate move will be towards greater surveillance; for better or for worse, companies will be watching and sometimes recording what their workforce does. The trend could take many different forms, from measuring body temperatures with thermal cameras to monitoring via an app how employees comply with social distancing."

It is evident we have fallen into a behavioral modification experiment. Jaron Lanier wrote *Ten Arguments for Deleting Your Social Media Accounts Right Now*. He notes that we are losing our free will because of algorithmic behavioral modification. He says, "We're being hypnotized little by little by technicians we can't see, for purposes we don't know. We're all lab animals now." Mr. Lanier's book lays out how we suddenly found ourselves in a new normal of "pervasive surveillance and constant, subtle manipulation—which is unethical, cruel, dangerous and inhumane." Mr. Lanier refers to the social media empires as "Behavioral Modification Empires."

Sean Parker, the First President of Facebook, has said, "We need to sort of give you a dopamine hit every once in a while, because someone liked or commented on a photo or a post or whatever...it's a social-validation feedback loop...exactly the kind of thing that a hacker like myself would come up with, because you're exploiting vulnerability in human psychology." Also, Chamath Palihapitiya, former Vice President of User Growth at Facebook, said the following, "The short-term, dopamine-driven feedback loops we've created are destroying how society works...no civil discourse, no cooperation; misinformation, mistruth."

Also, Jaron Lanier, from his book, writes, "So the problem isn't behavior modification in itself. The problem is relentless, robotic, ultimately meaningless behavior modification in the service of unseen manipulators and uncaring algorithms. Hypnosis might be therapeutic so long as you trust your hypnotist, but who would trust a hypnotist who is working for unknown third parties? Who? Apparently billions of people." We have now entered an alarming stage of groupthink. We are being herded like cattle. To make matters even worse, we have the equivalent of herding dogs due in part to an industry in counterfeit humans. According to the *New York Times*, the going rate for fake people on Twitter in early 2018 was $225 for the first 25,000 fake followers. These fake people are bots that are in many ways powered by Artificial Intelligence. Even the companies that sell counterfeit people are often fake themselves. This leads to massive simulated social media activities that influence real people. Then we wonder why we feel as if we are living in an alternate reality. Perhaps it may have something to do with the fact that we are not even interacting with real people but a pre-programmed agenda powered by bots to manipulate our thoughts.

To make matters even more stunning, Shoshana Zuboff, author of the book *The Age of Surveillance Capitalism*, in an independent documentary, highlighted Facebook's massive "Contagion Experiments." In the documentary, Zuboff said that Facebook, in these "Contagion Experiments," used subliminal cues and language manipulation to see if they could make people feel happier or sadder and affect real-world behavior offline. As it turns out, they can. Two key findings from those experiments were:

1. Manipulating language and inserting subliminal cues in the online context can change real-world behavior and emotion.
2. These methods and powers can be exercised "while bypassing user awareness."

In the documentary, Zuboff also explains how the Pokemon Go online game—which Google created, was engineered to manipulate real-world behavior and profit activity. She also describes the scheme in her *New York Times* article, saying: "Game players did not know that they were pawns in the real game of behavior modification for profit, as the rewards and punishments of hunting imaginary creatures were used to herd people to the McDonald's, Starbucks and local pizza joints that were paying the company for 'football,' in exactly the same way the online advertisers pay for 'click-through' to their websites." We cannot help but point out that we may be living in the most significant "Contagion Experiment" of them all. The Covid-19 pandemic led to substantial sales and profits related to products purchased from hand sanitizer to face masks, face shields, and remedies of all sorts. Essentially, we are being manipulated every day in countless ways. As a result of hidden surveillance in our lives, we are being mined for data for these Social Media empires as if living in a dystopian novel.

Shoshana Zuboff, in her January 24, 2020, *New York Times* op-ed, states that "you are now remotely controlled. Surveillance capitalists control **the science and the scientists,** the secrets and the truth." She continues by saying, "We thought that we search Google, but now we understand that Google searches us. We assumed that we use social media to connect, but we learned that connection is how social media uses us." Google, with its associated data mining complete with pop-up advertisements, is a form of mental theft. Worse, we have not given Google or any other entity permission to invade our private mental space.

On the other hand, we ask God to search our hearts allowing us to retain our free will. We must pause and look at Psalm 139:23-25, which says, "Search me, O God, and know my heart! Try me and know my thoughts! And see if there be any grievous way in me, and lead me in the way everlasting!" Instead of God searching our hearts, it is the false god of Google searching our hearts and minds leading not to the way everlasting but to a mental prison camp filled with useless idols. Zuboff also writes, "Surveillance capitalists exploit the widening inequity of knowledge for the sake of profits. They manipulate the economy, our society, and even our lives with impunity, endangering not just individual privacy but democracy itself." Zuboff discusses something called "Epistemic Inequality," which refers to inequality in what you are able to learn. "It is defined as unequal access to learning imposed by private commercial mechanisms of information capture, production, analysis, and sales. It is best exemplified in the fast-growing abyss between what we know and what is known about us."

Further, Google, Facebook, Amazon, and Microsoft have spearheaded the surveillance market transformation, placing themselves at the top tier of the epistemic hierarchy. Zuboff continues in her *New York Times* op-ed, "They operated in the shadows to amass huge knowledge monopolies by taking without asking, a maneuver that every child recognizes as theft" and "Surveillance capitalism begins by unilaterally staking a claim to private human experience as free raw material for translation into behavioral data. Our lives are rendered as data flows." The technocratic elites have turned us into lab animals and a commodity to be manipulated through data harvesting and artificial intelligence through these data flows. We are now the puppets on a string dancing to the Orwellian orchestra of techno-tyrants and profiteers. Shoshana Zuboff writes, "Now people have become targets for remote control, as surveillance capitalists discovered that the most predictive data come from intervening in behavior to tune, herd and modify actions in the direction of commercial objectives."

In 2010, Nicholas Carr wrote the *New York Times* bestselling book *The Shallows: What the Internet Is Doing to Our Brains*. This is a ground-breaking book that delves into the impact of internet usage on individuals and society. In his book, Carr delves into what he calls the Juggler's Brain, informing us that "when we go online, we enter an environment that promotes cursory reading, hurried and distracted thinking, and superficial learning." Carr also states that "it also turns us into lab rats constantly pushing levers to get tiny pellets of social and intellectual nourishment." He also adds that "our use of the Internet involves many paradoxes, but the one that promises to have the greatest long-term influence over how we think is this one: the Net seizes our attention only to scatter it. We focus intensively on the medium itself, on the flickering screen, but we're distracted by the medium's rapid-fire delivery of competing messages and stimuli." Many psychologists, neurobiologists, and educators say that heavy use of the Internet and Social Media has neurological consequences.

Carr also writes in his book that "The Net is, by design, an interruption system, a machine geared for dividing attention." Ziming Liu, a library science professor at San Jose State University, has stated that "the advent of digital media and the growing collection of digital documents have had a profound impact on reading." The findings, said Liu, indicate that "the digital environment tends to encourage people to explore many topics extensively, but at a more superficial level," and that "hyperlinks distract people from reading and thinking deeply." Liu states that a "screen-based reading behavior is emerging," which is characterized by "browsing and scanning, keyword spotting, one-time reading, and non-linear reading." The time "spent on in-depth reading and concentrated reading" is, on the *other hand, falling steadily.*

Nicholas Carr adds, based on his research on the impact of the Internet on people's brains, that "given our brain's plasticity, we know that our online habits continue to reverberate in the workings of our synapses when we're not online. We can assume that the neural circuits devoted to scanning, skimming, and multitasking are expanding and strengthening, while those used for reading and thinking deeply, with sustained concentration, are weakening or eroding." Carr adds further that "every click we make on the Web marks a break in our concentration, a bottom-up disruption of our attention—and it's in Google's economic interest to make sure we click as often as possible. The last thing the company wants is to encourage leisurely reading or slow, concentrated thought. Google is, quite literally, in the business of distraction." Worse, Don Tapscott, the technology writer, puts it more bluntly. Now that we can look up anything "with a click on Google," he says, "memorizing long passages or historical facts" is obsolete. Memorization is "a waste of time."

Carr cites Gunther Anders, the twentieth-century philosopher who said, "Everything that human beings are doing to make it easier to operate computer networks is at the same time, but for different reasons, making it easier for computer networks to operate human beings." Lastly, Carr refers to George Dyson, who wrote *Darwin Among the Machines* in 1997 related to artificial intelligence. Dyson was invited to Googleplex and left very troubled, writing the following, "I thought the coziness to be almost overwhelming. Happy Golden Retrievers running in slow motion through water sprinklers on the lawn. People waving and smiling, toys everywhere. I immediately suspected that unimaginable evil was happening somewhere in the dark corners. If the devil would come to earth, what place would be better to hide?" Carr adds that his "reaction, though obviously extreme, is understandable. With its enormous ambition, its immense bankroll, and its imperialistic designs on the world of knowledge, Google is a natural vessel for our fears as well as our hopes." "Some say Google is God," Sergey Brin of Google has acknowledged. "Others say Google is Satan."

The contagion virus was used to create a "Contagion Experiment" designed to further control the populace due to the Internet withering of our mental faculties. We find ourselves part of a contagion within a contagion intended to confuse and deceive, creating reckless endangerment to countless lives. Discernment and wisdom are now from a bygone age, leaving us with minds like desperate vagabonds searching for social media satisfaction.

The idols of science entice us while our souls are being corrupted by false promises of safety from a media-manufactured contagion. 1 Thessalonians 5:3 says, "For when they say, 'Peace and safety!' then sudden destruction comes upon them, as labor pains upon a pregnant woman. And they shall not escape." As Christians, we are called into prayer, supplication, fasting, and meditation. We must take time fasting from the Internet, social media, smartphones, tablets, and television. We must return to the biblical practice of meditating on God's Word and removing ourselves from a dystopian world constructed with behavioral algorithms, surveillance, and technocrats seeking to turn us into mindless, robotic consumers and pawns for their dominance. Puritan John Ball wrote in his book, *Divine Meditation*, "Meditation is serious, earnest and purposed musing upon some point of Christian instruction, tending to lead us forward toward the Kingdom of Heaven, and serving our daily strengthening against the flesh, the world, and the devil." We must find time to separate ourselves from the world and focus on the Word of God. This battle is tremendous, and our minds have been paralyzed by fear because of the Covid-19 pandemic and not by the comforting promises of the Word of God. Scripture makes clear that fear is not of the Spirit of God. Therefore, this fear comes from a well-designed plan manipulating us to give up our freedoms and liberties for the perception of safety, leading to relentless global tyranny that has only just begun. Joshua 1:8 says, "This Book of the Law shall not depart from your mouth, but you shall meditate on it day and night, so that you may be careful to do according to all that is written in it. For then you will make your way prosperous, and then you will have good success." This battle can only be won by the Word of God, the Lord Jesus Christ, and His Holy Spirit that renews our hearts and our minds.

"Their idols are silver and gold,
the work of human hands.
They have mouths, but do not speak;
eyes, but do not see.
They have ears, but do not hear;
noses, but do not smell.
They have hands, but do not feel;
feet, but do not walk;
and they do not make a sound in their throat.
Those who make them become like them;
so do all who trust in them."
Psalm 115:4-8

"To remain vital, culture must be renewed in the minds of the members
of every generation. Outsource memory, and culture withers."
Nicholas Carr—The Shallows

THE MASK OF GOD

"You cannot see my face, for man shall not see me and live."
Exodus 33:20 (ESV)

"What else is all our work to God – whether in the fields, in the garden, in the city, in the house, in war, or in government—but the work of children, by which He wants to give His gifts in the fields, at home, and everywhere else? These are the masks of God, behind which he wants to remain concealed and do all things."
Martin Luther

T HE COVID-19 pandemic witnessed unprecedented acts of medical tyranny involving egregious lockdowns, social distancing, and the wearing of masks as if making us all participants in a drama from an ancient play without end. We were told that certain businesses were essential and others non-essential while the techno-tyrants consolidated their wealth by taking over the functions of the small business class. More devastating was the loss of employment, a further desecration of private property, and the way God functions in our world.

In his book, *Under the Influence: How Christianity Transformed Civilization*, Alvin Schmidt writes, "The high value that Christianity assigned to work and manual labor received further support during the Reformation, especially from Martin Luther, who saw work not only as God-pleasing but also as a calling (vocation) to serve God. . . . Work was not an end in itself but something the person did in everyday life to the glory of God and to the service of mankind. . . . Luther saw work as the 'Mask of God' (larvae Dei), meaning that God is in it, although hidden.

So hidden is God in one's work that unless the Christian thinks about it (and only the Christian, with the Spirit of God in him, can do so), he will have no awareness of God's presence in his work. Given that God is hidden in one's work, to the Christian, all work is of equal value."

Further, Gene Veith, in his book *God at Work: Your Christian Vocation in All of Life*, writes, "Luther goes so far as to say that vocation is a mask of God. That is, God hides Himself in the workplace, the family, the Church, and secular society. To speak of God being hidden is a way of describing His presence, as when a child hiding in the room is there, just not seen. To realize that the mundane activities that take up most of our lives—going to work, taking the kids to soccer practice, picking up a few things at the store, going to Church—are hiding places for God can be a revelation in itself. Most people seek God in mystical experiences, spectacular miracles, and extraordinary acts they have to do. To find Him in vocation brings Him, literally, down to earth, makes us see how close He really is to us, and transfigures everyday life." It is evident that these areas are now being attacked as a result of the Great Reset both here in the United States and abroad.

Darrow L. Miller wrote in his book *Life Work* that "the Reformers of the Protestant movement recognized the importance of our economic lives as citizens of God's kingdom." Further, he states that "it was the biblical worldview taught by the Reformers that economic historians have recognized as a major factor in lifting whole nations out of poverty through the development of middle-class society. Through the new economies of Europe, multitudes were freed to live a life very different from that of the old indentured servants and serfs, to enjoy broader opportunities in their lives, and to have a significant effect on the life of the nation."

The idea of the "Mask of God" came from Martin Luther's understanding of Exodus 33:20, "You cannot see my face, for man shall not see me and live." Because of man's sin nature, human beings cannot see God in His transcendent nature and survive. Luther's theology extends to the mask of mercy, the mask of family, and the mask of evangelism. The Mask of God is how God accomplishes His purposes for the world. Nothing is secular to God, for He uses it all to fulfill His grand love story for the world. It should now be evident that anything that stands in the way of employment, whether working on a pipeline or being a self-employed business owner, is a violation of our God-given nature to work and be productive. Our right to work is part of our private property rights and individual freedom. Both are rooted in two of the Ten Commandments, "You shall not steal" and "You shall not covet." Both assume that an individual has the right to acquire property and to do as he pleases at his discretion, all under the authority of God's Word.

Gene Veith summarizes Luther's view: "When I go into a restaurant, the waitress who brings me my meal, the cook in the back who prepared it, the delivery men, the wholesalers, the workers in the food-processing factories, the butchers, the farmers, the ranchers, and everyone else in the economic food chain are all being used by God to 'give me this day my daily bread.' This is the doctrine of vocation. God works through people, in their ordinary stations of life to which He has called them, to care for His creation. In this way, He cares for everyone Christian and non-Christian whom He has given life. [As Luther puts it,] vocations are 'Masks of God.' On the surface, we see an ordinary human face, our mother, the doctor, the teacher, the waitress, our pastor, but, beneath the appearances, God is ministering to us through them. God is hidden in human vocations. The other side of the coin is that God is hidden in us. When we live out our callings as spouses, parents, children, employers, employees, citizens, and the rest, God is working through us. Even when we do not realize it, when we fulfill our callings, we too are Masks of God." Further, Martin Luther says the following, "God is the giver of all good gifts; but you must fall to, and take the bull by the horns, which means you must work to give God an occasion and a mask."

Over the last year, we have seen an insidious violation of private property rights by dictating how restaurant owners and other businesses operate. This strikes against the "Mask of God," disrupting the hidden and seen order of things. **Martin Luther wrote, "Thus God wears the mask of the Devil, and the Devil wears the mask of God; God wants to be** recognized under the mask of the Devil, and he wants the Devil to be condemned under the mask of God." The "Mask of God" is far different than the ones required by men during a pandemic. The masks we find ourselves wearing are counterfeit and turn us into gagged slaves. These masks are a mockery of the real Mask of God. Perhaps, these masks are veiling a hidden agenda for the Great Reset and the feudalistic conquest of a few returning us to the days of free men versus slaves. Although these artificial masks abound, the Works of God continue. He is now a mask hidden behind a mask fulfilling all of His plans and purposes by taking a counterfeit mask and making it His own. For it is only the "Mask of God" that works through our labors, whatever they may be, bringing glory and honor to His Kingdom.

There are even further implications to the masks we wear that involve our relationship to the Lord Jesus Christ. We must understand that God created the face to reflect His Glory. We find Moses veiled during the Old Testament, and He could not see God's Face and live. The Holy of Holies was veiled, for we could not get near to God. Although God was concealed during this time of man's history, He would be revealed during the witness of the Lord Jesus Christ, who is God Incarnate. At His Cruci-fixion, the veil in the Temple was torn in two. We read in 2 Corinthians 3:18, "And we all, with unveiled face, beholding the Glory of the Lord, are being transformed into the same image from one degree of glory to another. For this comes from the Lord who is the Spirit."

Further, in 2 Corinthians 4:6, we read, "For God, who said, 'Let light shine out of darkness,' has shone in our hearts to give the light of the knowledge of the Glory of God in the face of Jesus Christ." We see in these passages that to have the full knowledge of God, we do so with an unveiled face. We come to the Lord without fear of death. We are His image-bearers sharing the message of the Gospel. Our faces can also con-vey wordless messages by silent expressions relating our joy, contentment, and hope for eternity. Now our unveiled faces were masked, a heinous crime against the Gospel of the Lord Jesus Christ. We who have been made alive in Christ are not designed to be masked in fear by those in power who seek our subjugation. We submit ourselves only to the Lord Jesus Christ and not a state of tyranny. It all has been a veiled attempt at concealing the Gospel by the mask of the Devil.

In his book *Ezekiel*, Robert W. Jenson writes the following: "In ancient drama, the actors brought the gods and heroes into the theatre by and as masks by which the actors hid and through which they spoke; within the ceremony the masks were dramatis personae. Martin Luther adduced this phenomenon, but reversed the relation of actors and masks. God brings the created heroes and villains of the temporal drama onto history's stage as masks that hide him—for were he to appear barefaced, creation would perish. Thus Nebuchadnezzar and his like are larvae Dei, God's Masks—as indeed are all creatures in one way or another, and we masks truly are the personae of the drama; we are not puppets manipulated by someone distant from us. Yet behind us hides the Creator."

Although we are physically hidden behind literal masks, we are not puppets to men and their worldly policies. We are part of the Logos, which defines our calling in every one of us. We must remember that both heroes and villains are the Masks of God playing their part in a grand Cosmic drama that will one day usher in the real Great Reset when the Lord Jesus Christ returns condemning the mask of the Devil once and for all under the Mask of God.

"Watch, stand fast in the faith, be brave, be strong."
1 Corinthians 13

"But you must adhere to and follow this sure and infallible rule: God in His divine wisdom arranges to manifest Himself to human beings by some definite and visible form which can be seen with the eyes and touched with the hands, in short, is within the scope of the five senses. So near to us does the Divine majesty place itself."
Martin Luther

THE GREAT COUNTERFEIT FRACTIONAL RESERVE BANKING

"Counterfeiting, therefore, is inflationary, redistributive, distorts the economic system, and amounts to stealthy and insidious robbery and expropriation of all legitimate property-owners in society."
Murray Rothbard—The Case Against the Fed

"Where did the money come from? It came—and this is the most important single thing to know about modern banking— it came out of thin air. Commercial banks—that is, fractional reserve banks, create money out of thin air."
Murray Rothbard

"Your silver has become dross, your best wine mixed with water."
Isaiah 1:22

I**T IS NOW** time to reveal to our readers the deceptive and flawed foundation of our entire banking system. From the ancient days, since the fateful words by the deceiver "did God really say" were uttered, man has found himself in rebellion against God. Because of this rebellious nature resulting from the fall, man would prefer to be subjugated through tyranny rather than liberty found in submission to the authority and ordinances of God. We read in 1 Samuel 8:4-19, "Then all the elders of Israel gathered together and came to Samuel at Ramah and said to him, 'Behold, you are old and your sons do not walk in your ways. Now appoint for us a king to judge us like all the nations.' But the thing displeased

Samuel when they said, 'Give us a king to judge us.' And Samuel prayed to the Lord. And the Lord said to Samuel, 'Obey the voice of the people in all that they say to you, for they have not rejected you, but they have rejected me from being king over them. According to all the deeds that they have done, from the day I brought them up out of Egypt even to this day, forsaking me and serving other gods, so they are also doing to you. Now then, obey their voice; only you shall solemnly warn them and show them the ways of the king who shall reign over them.' So Samuel told all the words of the Lord to the people who were asking for a king from him. He said, 'These will be the ways of the king who will reign over you: he will take your sons and appoint them to his chariots and to be his horsemen and to run before his chariots. And he will appoint for himself commanders of thousands and commanders of fifties, and some to plow his ground and to reap his harvest, and to make his implements of war and the equipment of his chariots. He will take your daughters to be perfumers and cooks and bakers. He will take the best of your fields and vineyards and olive orchards and give them to his servants. He will take the tenth of your grain and of your vineyards and give it to his officers and to his servants. He will take your male servants and female servants and the best of your young men and your donkeys, and put them to his work. He will take the tenth of your flocks, and you shall be his slaves. And in that day you will cry out because of your king, whom you have chosen for yourselves, but the Lord will not answer you in that day.' But the people refused to obey the voice of Samuel. And they said, 'No! But there shall be a king over us.'" We have seen it unfold through history: conscription for wars, ongoing violations of private property rights, taxation, bread and circuses, and the inevitable debasement of the currency. Because man desires to be like God, he is inclined to establish government acting as the supreme ruler. However, this government is limited to the extent of man's finite nature. Therefore, a mechanism must be created to imitate what only God can do. This mechanism is designed to create something out of nothing. Without man knowing, this very mechanism will put him into bondage to the state. In addition, through its exact function, this mechanism will also imitate God's redemptive power through false provision and redistribution of wealth. This mechanism is the Great Counterfeit known as fractional reserve banking.

In Leviticus 19:35-36, we read, "You shall do no wrong in judgment, in measures of length or weight or quantity. You shall have just balances, just weights, a just ephah, and a just hin: I am the Lord your God, who brought you out of the land of Egypt." This scripture is God's ordinance to maintain honest money to facilitate a functioning economy. Sadly, man seeks to manipulate others through the economy and control of the currency. Far worse, moral debasement is reflected in monetary debasement. Corruption and theft begin in the heart, and then it corrupts and steals everything around it. In Isaiah 1:21-25, we read, "How the faithful city has become a whore, she who was full of justice! Righteousness lodged in her, but now murderers. **Your silver has become dross**, your best wine mixed with water. Your princes are rebels and companions of thieves. Everyone loves a bribe and runs after gifts. They do not bring justice to the fatherless, and the widow's cause does not come to them. Therefore the Lord declares, the Lord of hosts, the Mighty One of Israel: 'Ah, I will get relief from my enemies and avenge myself on my foes. I will turn my hand against you and will smelt away your dross as with lye and remove all your alloy.'" The silver became dross over time due to adding other metals to it. This is the process of debasing a currency which leads to inflation. This level of debasement is nothing compared to our current monetary system, which has no backing of gold or silver. All of our currency is dross. It is of interest to point out that our currency is called Fiat. Fiat is defined as a declaration by supreme law or a formal authorization, a command. Whose supreme law? Whose command? Very simply put, Fiat is a government-issued currency. It is man playing the supreme ruler through the mechanism of money and fractional reserve banking. John Maynard Keynes said, "There is no subtler or surer means of overturning the existing basis of society than to debauch the currency. The process engages all the hidden forces of economic law on the side of destruction and does it in a manner which not one man in a million is able to diagnose."

To demonstrate the counterfeit of fractional reserve banking, we first must turn to scripture. In Exodus 22:26-27, we read, "If ever you take your neighbor's cloak in pledge, you shall return it to him before the sun goes down, for that is his only covering, and it is his cloak for his body; in what else shall he sleep? And if he cries to me, I will hear, for I am compassionate." Here we see a person of very simple means who needs to take a loan and put up his cloak as collateral. However, what if this individual put up the same cloak ten times? This use of collateral would be considered multiple indebtedness, which violates biblical principles. Fractional reserve banking is multiple indebtedness.

Now let's illustrate this. You go to your local bank and deposit $100. The bank, in turn, gives you a receipt in the form of a bank deposit slip. The bank then takes $10 and sends it to the Federal Reserve Bank to meet their reserve requirement. The bank then loans out the remaining $90; the person who borrows the $90 deposits it in his bank. His bank takes $9 and sends it to the Federal Reserve to meet the reserve requirement. This process continues throughout the entire economic system. In his book *The Case Against the Fed*, Murray Rothbard said the following: "Let us see how this process typically works. Suppose the 'money multiplier'— the multiple that commercial banks can pyramid on top of reserves, is 10:1. The multiple is the inverse of the Fed's legally imposed minimum reserve requirement on different types of banks, a minimum which now approximates 10 percent. Almost always, if banks can expand 10:1 on top of their reserves, they will do so since that is how they make their money. The counterfeiter, after all, will strongly tend to counterfeit as much as he can legally get away with. Suppose that the Fed decides it wishes to expand the nation's total money supply by $10 billion. If the money multiplier is ten, then the Fed will choose to purchase $1 billion of assets, generally U.S. government securities, on the open market. Where did the Fed get the money to pay for those bonds? It created the money out of thin air, simply writing out a check on itself." Because borrowing is at the center of this scheme, money is created out of debt. What we think is money is an illusion built on debt.

In his book *The Creature from Jekyll Island*, G. Edward Griffin writes, "By calling those bonds 'reserves,' the Fed then uses them as the base for creating nine additional dollars for every dollar created for the bonds themselves. The money created for the bonds is spent by the government, whereas the money created on top of those bonds is the source of all the bank loans made to the nation's businesses and individuals. The result of this process is the same as creating money on a printing press, but the illusion is based on an accounting trick rather than a printing trick. The bottom line is that Congress and the banking cartel have entered into a partnership in which the cartel has the privilege of collecting interest on money which it creates out of nothing, a perpetual override on every American dollar that exists in the world. Congress, on the other hand, has access to unlimited funding without having to tell the voters their taxes are being raised through the process of inflation." This is the entirety of fractional reserve banking and the reality of the Great Counterfeit.

Further, Keynesian economics has led to government policies encouraging debt with tax deductions for interest, discouraging savings. All of this leads to financial repression. Since the Federal Reserve Act of 1913 (a protection racket for counterfeiters), we have seen the rise of the military-industrial complex, a debauched currency leading to inflation, taxation, distortion of the business cycle leading to numerous economic booms and busts such as the 1930's depression and the 2008-2009 mortgage crisis. When the system is shocked, as we saw during the Covid-19 pandemic, it allows the government through deficit spending to further consolidate control over the population leading to more and more government dependence. In the article "Government: The Good, the Bad, and the Ugly," Professor Paul Cleveland wrote, "The imposition of welfare policies in a nation is best understood in the context of socialism. In this country it would be the evolutionary form of socialism. That is, in an effort to eliminate property rights, socialists begin by proposing gradual policies of change. The implementation of welfare programs serves as a useful beginning for they undermine property rights. These policies **veil** the force of government **behind the mask of benevolence** even though the thrust of them is the gradual erosion of property rights and the development of socialism. Often the proposals are willingly accepted because their stated end is to alleviate the suffering of the poor." Keynesian economics allows for the transfer of wealth through inflationary policies to the government. This economic destruction is socialism by stealth because the government now has at its disposal money created out of thin air. Welcome to the Central Bank of Communism.

Proverbs 20:23 says, "Unequal weights are an abomination to the Lord, and false scales are not good." Our monetary system reflects our rebellion against God and our sinful nature. False weights and measures lead to unrighteousness, fraud, counterfeiting and tyranny. Society created a false god when we demanded a king to rule over us other than the one true living God. A false god that imitates without success only what God can do. As a result of fractional reserve banking America is living in an illusion of affluent poverty. The Great Counterfeit has led not to liberty and freedom but to bondage and captivity.

> *"Shall I acquit the man with wicked scales*
> *and with a bag of deceitful weights?*
> *Your rich men are full of violence;*
> *your inhabitants speak lies,*
> *and their tongue is deceitful in their mouth.*
> *Therefore I strike you with a grievous blow,*
> *making you desolate because of your sins.*
> *You shall eat, but not be satisfied,*
> *and there shall be hunger within you;*
> *you shall put away, but not preserve,*
> *and what you preserve I will give to the sword.*
> *You shall sow, but not reap;*
> *you shall tread olives, but not anoint yourselves with oil;*
> *you shall tread grapes, but not drink wine."*
> Micah 6:11-15

IF THE FOUNDATIONS ARE DESTROYED, WHAT CAN THE RIGHTEOUS DO?

"In the Lord I take refuge;
how can you say to my soul,
'Flee like a bird to your mountain,
for behold, the wicked bend the bow;
they have fitted their arrow to the string
to shoot in the dark at the upright in heart;
if the foundations are destroyed,
what can the righteous do?'"

"The Lord is in his holy temple;
the Lord's throne is in heaven;
his eyes see, his eyelids test the children of man.
The Lord tests the righteous,
but his soul hates the wicked and the one who loves violence.
Let him rain coals on the wicked;
fire and sulfur, and a scorching wind shall be the portion of their cup.
For the Lord is righteous;
he loves righteous deeds;
the upright shall behold his face."
Psalm 11 (ESV)

W E HAVE BEEN told it would be fourteen days to flatten the curve, which as of this writing is now well over eighty weeks with no end in sight. Psalm 11, in many translations, is known as the Song of the Steadfast.

We look at the words from Psalm 11:3, which says, "If the foundations are destroyed, what can the righteous do?" Today we see the foundations all around us being torn down in upheaval both politically and economically. Albert Barnes writes regarding the destruction of the foundations the following: "The reference is to the destruction of those things in a community, when the truth is no longer respected; when justice is no longer practiced; when fraud and violence have taken the place of honesty and honor; when error prevails; when a character for integrity and virtue affords no longer any security. This is supposed to be the case in the circumstances referred to in the Psalm, when there was no respect paid to truth and justice, and when the righteous, therefore, could find no security."

In this Psalm, David's faith in the Lord is being questioned by those around him, and he is being advised to "flee like a bird to your mountain." How many of us have a small voice in our minds that is instructing us to flee? By that, it could mean not facing the reality we are living in or withdrawing from the Word of God, or we have a temptation in our heart to distrust God thinking we can rely on our own understanding to get through this "new normal" we find ourselves. Many of us are like David, and we are in fear because of an uncertain future. Many wonder what further damage is in store to the economy and employment. Matthew Henry gives us comfort when he comments on this Psalm by saying, "Those that truly fear God and serve him are welcome to put their trust in him. The psalmist, before he gives an account of his temptation to distrust God, records his resolution to trust in Him, as that by which he was resolved to live and die. The believer, though not terrified by his enemies, may be tempted, **by the fears of his friends, to desert his post, or neglect his work**. They perceive his danger but not his security; they give him counsel that **savors of worldly policy** rather than of **heavenly wisdom**. The principles of religion are the foundations on which the faith and hope of the righteous are built. We are concerned to hold these fast against all temptations to unbelief, for believers would be undone if they had not God to go to, God to trust in, and future bliss to hope for. The prosperity of wicked people in their wicked, evil ways, and the straits and distresses which the best men are sometimes brought into, tried David's faith." David's faith was tried. David was being **demoralized** by the pressures of wicked desires and evil ambitions all around him. Yet David triumphed because he trusted in the Lord's sovereignty over all things.

Now more than ever is the time that we must draw nearer to the Lord and the Foundation of His Principles that can never be destroyed. During this time of economic uncertainty, believers must turn their attention toward the biblical principles of money management, stewardship, and the dignity of work and not the council of worldly policy that is not aligned with a biblical worldview. It was the Christian faith that elevated man to economic dignity and freedom. It was the Christian faith and worldview that created the middle class. Before the transformative power of Christianity, there were two classes of people; free men and slaves who did manual labor. In his book *Under the Influence: How Christianity Transformed Civilization*, Alvin Schmidt wrote, "Before Christians brought dignity to work and labor, there was not much of a middle class in the Greek or Roman cultures. People were either rich or poor, and the poor were commonly slaves. The Christian emphasis on everyone being required to work and work being honorable and God-pleasing had the effect of producing a class between the patricians (the wealthy) and the plebes (the poor)."

Because of our current culture and the syncretism creeping into the true meaning of stewardship, we are returning to the pagan days of patricians and plebes. The decadence of paganism is destroying the true foundations built on a Christian worldview. It can also be said that some of these foundations we see being destroyed are but idols that man has created. The idol of mammon has become a false god through an economic system built on a great counterfeit. The foundation of our economic system is not a foundation at all but a financial tower of Babel built on the illusion of abundance and wealth. A counterfeit that imitates only what the one true living God can do, creating something out of nothing. This counterfeit god can only do so through an inflationary process that leads to the bondage of debt. Then with the sleight of hand of monetary alchemy and government oversight, they imitate the redemptive power of God through all their redistribution of wealth schemes. In Hosea 8:4, we read, "They made idols for their own destruction." America and the world are nearing destruction while worshipping these false gods.

Now is the time that we must look closely at the foundations of our own lives. Are they crumbling all around us? And if so, what sort of foundation have we built for ourselves? For without the foundations of God, nothing can withstand the storms of life. For those who keep His covenants, He gives us confidence and strength in the words of Psalm 145:14-16, "The Lord upholds all who are falling and raises up all who are bowed down. The eyes of all look to you, and you give them their food in due season. You open your hand; you satisfy the desire of every living thing." When our personal and economic lives are built on the foundation of the Word of God, we do not succumb to principalities and powers that sweep us away, for we are secure in Him.

There is only one foundation, as Paul says in 1 Corinthians 3:11, "For no one can lay a foundation other than that which is laid, which is Jesus Christ." We read in Isaiah 28:16, "Therefore thus says the Lord God: Behold, I lay in Zion a stone for a foundation, a tried stone, a sure foundation; Whoever believes will not act hastily." Further, in Ephesians 2:20-21, we read, "Built on the foundation of the apostles and prophets, Christ Jesus Himself being the cornerstone, in whom the whole structure, being joined together, grows into a holy temple in the Lord." Jesus Christ is the Chief Cornerstone, an immovable cornerstone that supports the foundations of our lives and our economies. A foundation that holds everything together and a foundation that sustains and bears the burdens of this fractured creation.

Build on the Rock

"Therefore whoever hears these sayings of Mine, and does them, I will liken him to a wise man who built his house on the rock: and the rain descended, the floods came, and the winds blew and beat

on that house; and it did not fall, for it was founded on the rock.
But everyone who hears these sayings of Mine, and does not do
them, will be like a foolish man who built his house on the sand:
and the rain descended, the floods came, and the winds blew
and beat on that house, and it fell. And great was its fall."

Jesus Christ—Matthew 7:24-27

THE CHRISTIAN'S RESPONSE
TO AN ECONOMIC CRISIS

TODAY WE ARE dealing with circumstances involving a virus pandemic that is impacting both the markets and the economy. The shock of this virus pandemic has created a ripple effect through our lives and especially the economy as a whole. To understand the nature of this ripple effect, we must first and foremost understand how God designed the economy to work and how it has gone wrong. The foundation of God's economic system is found in Genesis 1:1, which says, "In the beginning, God created the heavens and the earth," and Genesis 1:26, which says, "Let us make man in our image, after our likeness. And let them have dominion over the fish of the sea and over the birds of the heavens and over the livestock and over all the earth and over every creeping thing that creeps on the earth." Many today cannot see the foundation of true economics in this passage. However, by understanding the creation account, we can construct the Ideal Economy by which humanity can thrive and prosper.

God created the earth, and God has appointed man to have dominion over it. Humans are created in God's image. God has designed the earth to respond and yield to humanity its fruits and all its gifts. God gave man the mission to take these resources, which have been given as a gift and move them to a higher level. Man takes things of a lower value and brings them to a higher value. In turn, the earth by God's design yields to man, and man, through his productivity, causes the earth to yield even more. God also created male and female to be fruitful and multiply and yield new generations. Man and nature are compatible because of God's creative design. As we adhere to God's principles, we see an economy that works well and leads to investments based on productivity. These investments become the seeds of capital that are added back into productive activity. This is called a virtuous cycle in which ethical behavior creates conditions for better behavior in the future. The key to this cycle working is giving back to the Creator to calibrate our hearts and minds to the reality of this system. Malachi 3:10 says, "Bring the full tithe into the storehouse, that there may be food in my house. And thereby put me to the test, says the Lord of hosts, if I will not open the windows of heaven for you and pour down for you a blessing until there is no more need." The most economically productive thing we can do is give from the first fruits of our labor. It provides us with the ability to acknowledge God as the one who owns it all and make Him Sovereign over our lives.

The dominion of man on earth is built on this cycle as created by God. With man's productivity comes choices between consumption and investment. Reinforcing this productivity is a work ethic that further enhances our productivity. As man forgoes consumption and saves, these savings are turned into investments. These investments are then put back into production, expanding society's wealth. From the wealth of society comes forth giving and generosity elevating those in need.

So, what has gone wrong with our economic system? Why doesn't it function as originally intended? The answer lies in the alienation of man from God. This alienation from God interrupts the virtuous cycle of the earth, man, productivity, and the capital markets. When the dominion of man is not understood from a biblical worldview, we underestimate man's ability to be productive when entering various forms of enterprise. When God, the Creator, is removed from the cycle, that is when this system breaks down. Suddenly, productivity, wealth, and investment are reduced, and man sees all around him scarcity, not the abundant plan of God the Creator. From this scarcity, anxiety takes hold, and as anxiety increases, it causes consumption to increase to fill the void left by God. Yet God's Word says in Philippians 4:6-7, "Do not be anxious about anything, but in everything by prayer and supplication with thanksgiving, let your requests be made known to God. And the peace of God, which surpasses all understanding, will guard your hearts and your minds in Christ Jesus."

In this dangerous state of anxiety, man, instead of turning toward God, pushes him away further. In his anxiousness, he seeks an alternative which the Bible calls Idols that we substitute for God. An idolatrous alternative that will restore the abundance and wealth of the system that only God Himself could create through His creative design and principles. Man establishes a counterfeit god called the government, which replaces the abundance and wealth of God's true economic system. To create this abundance and wealth, the government establishes a mechanism called the Federal Reserve to print money to create the appearance of this wealth. Productivity and the capital markets are now distorted. There are cycles of boom and bust. The money supply and related interest rates are manipulated, masking over the ability to assess risk. As money is continually introduced into the system, false wealth is created due to debt being used to further increase consumption due to man's anxiety. In turn, the government begins the process of confiscation through taxation, reducing further capital, investments, and giving, which could have gone elsewhere.

Once God is removed from all aspects of our society, we continue to push God out of the way and rely on our own understanding. Proverbs 3:5-7 says, "Trust in the Lord with all your heart, and do not lean on your own understanding. In all your ways, acknowledge him, and he will make straight your paths. Be not wise in your own eyes; fear the Lord, and turn away from evil." Because God is no longer at the center of our lives, everything becomes fragmented. This becomes a chain reaction whereby man is separated from production, and production is separated from the economic system. The system itself becomes fragmented. There is now a disconnect between investments and consumption, and this separates economics from the assessment of risk, which is known as interest rates. Modern Portfolio Theory, also known as Asset Allocation, ignores production and consumption. There is now a severed relationship between government action and investments. Wall Street operates on its own and focuses strictly on the markets themselves. Because Wall Street is running separately from production, markets are now emotionally driven, and people react out of anxiety, fear, and scarcity. Simply put, our markets and our economic systems are a mirror image of our fallen nature and fractured creation.

Some may question, especially during a time like this, where is God in all of this? The answer is that God has always been with us, and God created the perfect economic system for man to live. Perhaps the real question should be where man in all of this is? Has it not been humanity who relied on its own understanding and, in the process, erected false gods and idols to assuage their own inner anxieties due to its separation from God? Colossians 1:16-20 says, "For by him all things were created, in heaven and on earth, visible and invisible, whether thrones or dominions or rulers or authorities—all things were created through him and for him. And he is before all things, and in him, all things hold together. And he is the head of the body, the church. He is the beginning, the firstborn from the dead, that in everything he might be preeminent. For in him all the fullness of God was pleased to dwell, and through him to reconcile to himself all things, whether on earth or in heaven, making peace by the blood of his cross."

During times of crisis, this is the time when we are to draw near to God. During times of crisis, it is God's voice that calls us to His Word and for us to restore God's place of being first and foremost in our lives. It is not the government, nor is it man's contrived economic system that can save us. It is God through His Son, the Lord Jesus Christ, that brings us to salvation. God allows these things to occur so that we may see how He designed the perfect economy to be in harmony with humanity. During these times of crisis, we can see the transcendent principles of money management and stewardship, showing us the error of our ways and relying on our own understanding. Now is the time for Christians and non-Christians alike to look to the Word of God and submit themselves under the Authority of God and His Ideal Economy.

More importantly, now is the time that the Word of God and the Gospel of the Lord Jesus Christ be shared to get us through these trying times. Jesus Christ is the one who assuages our fears and brings all of humanity to salvation. Now is the time to bring the full tithe into the storehouse and fully trust in the Lord to be our provision.

I want to leave you with the words of Luke 8:23-25, "And as they sailed, he fell asleep. And a windstorm came down on the lake, and they were filling with water and were in danger. And they went and woke him, saying, 'Master, Master, we are perishing!' And he awoke and rebuked the wind and the raging waves, and they ceased, and there was a calm. He said to them, 'Where is your faith?' And they were afraid, and they marveled, saying to one another, 'Who then is this, that he commands even winds and water, and they obey him?'"

Focus on Jesus Christ and not the storm, for He is our rock, provision, and salvation!

THE BONDAGE OF DEBT

"The rich rules over the poor, and the
borrower is the slave of the lender."
Proverbs 22:7

"And forgive us our debts, as we
also have forgiven our debtors."
Jesus Christ—Matthew 6:12

"The Spirit of the Lord is upon me, because he has anointed me to
proclaim good news to the poor. He has sent me to proclaim liberty
to the captives and recovery of sight to the blind, to set at liberty
those who are oppressed, to proclaim the year of the Lord's favor."
Jesus Christ—Luke 4:18-19

FROM A PREVIOUS chapter, "The Great Counterfeit," we learned that Fractional Reserve Banking is anti-biblical and has led to inflationary policies and indebtedness. This is a form of bondage and, as can be seen around the world, leads to entire nations being subjected to financial repression and captivity. Michael Hudson, in his book *J Is For Junk Economics*, calls this debt peonage. He writes, "Debt peonage in today's post-industrial economy takes the form of obliging homebuyers, student debtors and others to spend their working lives paying off their mortgages, education loans, and other personal debts, which typically must be taken in order to survive."

The Bible warns of the use of debt. The Bible also discusses the use of debt Jubilees. In Leviticus 25:8-17, we read the following:

"You shall count seven weeks of years, seven times seven years, so that the time of the seven weeks of years shall give you forty-nine years. Then you shall sound the loud trumpet on the tenth day of the seventh month. On the Day of Atonement you shall sound the trumpet throughout all your land. And you shall consecrate the fiftieth year, and proclaim liberty throughout the land to all its inhabitants. It shall be a jubilee for you, when each of you shall return to his property and each of you shall return to his clan. That fiftieth year shall be a jubilee for you; in it you shall neither sow nor reap what grows of itself nor gather the grapes from the undressed vines. For it is a jubilee. It shall be holy to you. You may eat the produce of the field. In this year of jubilee each of you shall return to his property. And if you make a sale to your neighbor or buy from your neighbor, you shall not wrong one another. You shall pay your neighbor according to the number of years after the jubilee, and he shall sell to you according to the number of years for crops. If the years are many, you shall increase the price, and if the years are few, you shall reduce the price, for it is the number of the crops that he is selling to you. You shall not wrong one another, but you shall fear your God, for I am the Lord your God."

Also, in Deuteronomy 15:1-11, we read about something called the Shemittah year. "At the end of every seven years you shall grant a release. And this is the manner of the release: every creditor shall release what he has lent to his neighbor. He shall not exact it of his neighbor, his brother, because the Lord's release has been proclaimed. Of a foreigner you may exact it, but whatever of yours is with your brother your hand shall release. But there will be no poor among you; for the Lord will bless you in the land that the Lord your God is giving you for an inheritance to possess—if only you will strictly obey the voice of the Lord your God, being careful to do all this commandment that I command you today. For the Lord your God will bless you, as he promised you, and you shall lend to many nations, but you shall not borrow, and you shall rule over many nations, but they shall not rule over you. If among you, one of your brothers should become poor, in any of your towns within your land that the Lord your God is giving you, you shall not harden your heart or shut your hand against your poor brother, but you shall open your hand to him and lend him sufficient for his need, whatever it may be. Take care lest there be an unworthy thought in your heart and you say, 'The seventh year, the year of release is near,' and your eye look grudgingly on your poor brother, and you give him nothing, and he cry to the Lord against you, and you be guilty of sin. You shall give to him freely, and your heart shall not be grudging when you give to him, because for this the Lord your God will bless you in all your work and in all that you undertake. For there will never cease to be poor in the land. Therefore I command you, You shall open wide your hand to your brother, to the needy and to the poor, in your land."

What few know is that these debt releases were found throughout ancient history. In his book *And Forgive Them Their Debts*, Michael Hudson writes the following: "The idea of annulling debts nowadays seems so unthinkable that most economists and many theologians doubt whether the Jubilee Year could have been applied in practice, and indeed on a regular basis. A widespread impression is that the Mosaic debt Jubilee was a utopian ideal. However, Assyriologists have traced it to a long tradition of Near Eastern proclamations. That tradition is documented as soon as written inscriptions have been found in Sumer, starting in the mid-third millennium BC. Instead of causing economic crisis, Jubilees preserved stability in nearly all Near Eastern societies. Economic polarization, bondage and collapse occurred when such clean slates stopped being proclaimed." The objective of these debt Jubilees was to manage any potential control of the economic system by creditors. Hudson further states, "At the outset of recorded history, Bronze Age rulers relinquished fiscal claims and restored liberty from a permanent debt. That prevented a creditor oligarchy from emerging to the extent that occurred in classical antiquity. Today's world is still living in the wake of the Roman Empire's creditor-oriented laws and the economic polarization that ensued." Further, he states, "Something has to give when debts cannot be paid on a widespread basis. The volume of debt tends to increase exponentially, to the point where it causes a crisis. If debts are not written down, they will expand and become a lever for creditors to pry away land and income from the indebted economy at large. That is why debt cancellations to save rural economies from insolvency were deemed sacred from Sumer and Babylonia through the Bible."

The debt Jubilee and the seven-year Shemittah were designed to prevent severe economic polarization. Economic polarization leads to financial repression, subjugation, slavery, and authoritarian tyranny. Therefore, the burden of debt needed to be released through written ordinances. In addition, there is a specific Hebrew word deror used only seven times in scripture which denotes release leading to freedom. It is explicitly associated with the release of debt. Deror is found in Leviticus 25:10, Ezekiel 46:17, Isaiah 61:1, and four times in Jeremiah 34:8, 15, and 17 (twice). What we see in Jeremiah involves the promise of King Zedekiah to release the people's debts on the eve of the war with Babylonia in 588 BC. However, King Zedekiah went back on his word, ultimately leading to Judea's subsequent defeat. King Zedekiah broke his promise and violated the Word of God. Jeremiah 34:17 says, "Therefore, thus says the Lord: You have not obeyed me by proclaiming **liberty** (Deror—release of the debts), every one to his brother and to his neighbor; behold I proclaim to you **liberty** to the sword, to pestilence, and to famine, declares the Lord. I will make you a horror to all the kingdoms of the earth." As a result of the Israelites' 490 years of not adhering to the ordinances of the Shemittah and Jubilee, in addition to their apostasy and idolatry, they were sent into the Babylonian Captivity for seventy years. This would be the equivalent of seventy Shemittah years that occur every seven years. Therefore, seventy times seven is 490 years. In addition, Leviticus 25:10 says, "And you shall consecrate the fiftieth year, and proclaim **liberty** (Deror—release of the debts) throughout the land to all its inhabitants. It shall be a Jubilee for you, when each of you shall return to his property and each of you shall return to his clan."

In Luke 4:18-19 Jesus Christ says, "The Spirit of the Lord is upon me, because he has anointed me to proclaim good news to the poor.

He has sent me to proclaim **liberty** (Deror—release of the debts) to the captives and recovery of sight to the blind, to set at liberty those who are oppressed, to proclaim the year of the Lord's favor." Jesus is making a direct correlation to the Jubilee found in Isaiah 61:1, and by doing so, He is announcing the Jubilee. There is a two-fold meaning regarding debt. First is because of the fall of man, there is a debt regarding sin. Secondly, spiritual debt resulting from sin will manifest itself as financial debt. More importantly, during the time of Jesus, Rabbi Hillel instituted something called a Prosbul. In his book *The Temple*, Alfred Edersheim writes the following: "Rabbi Hillel devised a formula called the Prosbul, by which the rights of a creditor were fully secured. The Prosbul ran thus: I, A.B., give to you, the judges of C.D. (a declaration) to the effect that I may claim any debt due to me at whatever time I please. This Prosbul, signed by the judges or by witnesses, enabled a creditor to claim money lent even in the sabbatical year, and though professedly applying only to debts on real property, was so worded as to cover every case."

It is evident that through the use of judges and legislation, God's ordinances regarding the release of debts had now been circumvented, leading to the rise of a creditor class of elites who would rule over the poor and middle class of Judea. We can now see the significance of the passage of the Lord's Prayer that says, "And forgive us our debts, as we also have forgiven our debtors." It is clear that Jesus was very aware of the Prosbul, and it was this same type of behavior that led to Israel's captivity to the Babylonians. Further, in Matthew 26:11, Jesus says, "For you have the poor with you always, but Me you do not have always." Jesus is reinforcing the warning given to the Israelites from Deuteronomy 15:1-11. In his book *Jesus the Temple*, Nicholas Perrin writes the following: "For when Jesus says, you always have the poor with you, he is patently alluding to Deuteronomy 15:1-11, a passage in which Moses enjoins the seventh year as the year of canceling debts (Shemittah). The section of Deuteronomy is remarkable in its blend of idealism, realism, and pessimism. There will be no one in need among you, so the text promises, if only you will obey the Lord your God by diligently observing this entire commandment that I command you today. But, if there is among you anyone in need, the scripture continues on a less confident note, do not be hard-hearted or tight-fisted toward your needy neighbor." Jesus came as God Incarnate to proclaim release of sin and release those in captivity to debt. Jesus Christ is our Jubilee. In Matthew 18:21-22 (RSV), it says, "Then Peter came up and said to him, 'Lord, how often shall my brother sin against me, and I forgive him? As many as seven times?' Jesus said to him, 'I do not say to you seven times, but seventy times seven.'" Jesus is making a direct reference to the 490 years that the Israelites did not adhere to the release of the debts that led to their captivity. In addition, by using the words seventy times seven, we now turn our attention toward Daniel 9:24, which says, "Seventy weeks are decreed about your people and your holy city, to finish the transgression, to put an end to sin, and to atone for iniquity, to bring in everlasting righteousness, to seal both vision and prophet, and to anoint a most holy place." Once again, we see that seventy weeks of years is seventy times seven which is 490 years. Jesus Christ is the prophesied Messiah. He is the King of Kings and the Lord of Lords.

As a result of the Prosbul that was in force during the time of Jesus, another dangerous event would unfold thirty-three years after the Crucifixion of Christ. Many historians estimate that the Temple was completed in approximately 64 AD. That would imply that the building project would lead to unemployed workers. Jesus, during His ministry, was warning them about the dangers of debt. Few know that it was a debt revolt in 66 AD that was the flashpoint leading to the fall of Jerusalem in 70 AD. David A. Fiensy, in his book *Christian Origins and the Ancient Economy*, indicates that because of indebtedness, there was a debt revolt. He writes, "As is well known, Josephus does narrate one clear case of such an event in Palestine. In 66 AD during the Feast of Wood-Carrying, the Sicarii ("Dagger Carriers") and others broke forth into the upper city and set on fire the house of Ananias the High Priest and of Agrippa I and Berenice. Then the mob turned to the public buildings: After these things, they began to carry the fire to the archives, being zealous to destroy the contracts of those who had loaned money and to cancel the collection of debts. Josephus speculates at this point that the Sicarii hoped to win to their side a multitude of debtors." As we know from history, the situation did not diminish. The city of Jerusalem saw violence upon violence, famine, and pestilence. All were escalating to the point where the Romans leveled the city fulfilling the words of Jesus Christ in Mark 13:1-2, "And as He came out of the temple, one of His disciples said to him, 'Look teacher, what wonderful stones and what wonderful buildings!' And Jesus said to him, 'Do you see these great buildings?' There will not be left here one stone upon another that will not be thrown down."

What we see in our modern society is a predatory creditor oligarchy that now controls the lives of countless millions. Michael Hudson, in his book *Killing the Host—How Financial Parasites and Debt Destroy the Global Economy*, writes, "The political problem blocking debt write-downs is the one party's debts (mainly those of the 99 percent) are another's savings (especially those of the one percent). It is not possible to annul debts on the liabilities side of the balance sheet without wiping out savings on the asset side. As long as "savings" (mainly by the one percent) takes the form of debt claims on the rest of society, they will grow exponentially to hold the 99 percent in deepening debt thrall, monopolizing the surplus in a way that always shrinks the economy."

To think that the inscription on the Liberty Bell is from Leviticus 25:10, "Proclaim **Liberty** (Deror—release of the debts) throughout all the Land unto all the inhabitants thereof." Some of our Founding Fathers knew the perils of central banking and all that it would entail. Perhaps this is why the very verse they chose for the Liberty Bell refers to the Year of the Jubilee. Freedom in America would come from our inalienable rights under God the Creator as well as our freedom from the bondage of debt. As America began to remove God from all aspects of society, we've witnessed the destruction of our liberties and freedoms as we now descend into judgment and captivity.

"I sincerely believe that banking establishments are more dangerous than standing armies, and that the principle of spending money to be paid by posterity under the name of funding is but swindling futurity on a large scale."
Thomas Jefferson

"If the American people ever allow private banks to control the issue of their currency, first by inflation, then by deflation, the banks and corporations that will grow up around the banks will deprive the people of all property until their children wake up homeless on the continent their father conquered. The issuing power should be taken from the banks and restored to the people, to whom it properly belongs."
Thomas Jefferson

AMERICA'S CAPTIVITY

*"The only difference between a greedy man and an
adulterer is that one has an inordinate love for physical
form, the other a desire for a farm, a rich estate."*
Ambrose of Milan

*"Their property held them in chains. They think of themselves as owners,
whereas it is they rather who are owned. Enslaved as they are to their
own property, they are not the masters of their money but its slaves."*
Cyprian, Bishop of Carthage—Third Century

"It is when a people forget God that tyrants forge their chains."
Patrick Henry

TODAY AMERICA IS at a crucial time in its history. In this country, we
have seen the rise of central banking, which has imposed upon us a
creditor oligarchy. This creditor oligarchy works with the technocratic
elites tied into our government by manipulating social media and allowing for reckless censorship. In addition, we find ourselves in a nation of
affluent poverty because of our conspicuous and consumptive lifestyles.
This condition was spawned in many ways by John Maynard Keynes, who
sought to overthrow society by debauching the currency.

Further, Keynes began with a flawed premise that demand ultimately
will lead to the creation of supply. This premise would usher in nothing less
than debt-fueled consumption. This consumption through debt has led to
a provocation and condition of covetousness in many. This covetousness
is fueled even further by social media, making us feel inferior to what we

see, which is illusionary. Many have lost their bearings in determining how much is enough to satisfy them. Our culture, it seems, is gripped in the throes of dissatisfaction and discontentment. Because we do not recognize God's provision in our lives, we seek to find it for ourselves, leading to disappointment and emptiness. Our souls are empty as we seek to fill the void left by God with material solutions. When we look at the meaning of consumption, it indicates waste, destruction by burning, eating, devouring, scattering, and slow decay. America is devouring itself as it clings to nothing but the emptiness of illusions.

In many ways, the American Dream has turned into a debt-riddled nightmare. Although our currency says In God We Trust, the truth is it is money we trust, thus turning it into an idol of our hearts. A nation that prospers and achieves great wealth does so at the peril of forgetting that *God owns it all* and we are His Stewards. Without acknowledging the Lord and acting as His economic agents, we turn ourselves from stewards to slaves and lawless rebels. Yet, it is the Lord who has the power to give wealth, provided we are obedient to His precepts and His statutes. A nation that turns away from God in rebellion will worship the work of its own hands, idolizing itself, leading to enslavement. We find ourselves captive to the world through our lusts and desires, leading to a spiritual decay that spreads throughout the culture like a cancer. This cancer then metastasizes to the economy once and for all, bankrupting the nation. Our economy is merely a measure of how self-absorbed and prideful we are, holding up a mirror to our culture, revealing in its reflection how as a nation, we have walked away from God.

In Deuteronomy 28, we read the blessing for obedience to God: "And if you faithfully obey the voice of the Lord your God, being careful to do all his commandments that I command you today, the Lord your God will set you high above all the nations of the earth. And all these blessings shall come upon you and overtake you, if you obey the voice of the Lord your God. Blessed shall you be in the city, and blessed shall you be in the field. Blessed shall be the fruit of your womb and the fruit of your ground and the fruit of your cattle, the increase of your herds and the young of your flock. Blessed shall be your basket and your kneading bowl. Blessed shall you be when you come in, and blessed shall you be when you go out. The Lord will cause your enemies who rise against you to be defeated before you. They shall come out against you one way and flee before you seven ways. The Lord will command the blessing on you in your barns and in all that you undertake. And he will bless you in the land that the Lord your God is giving you. The Lord will establish you as a people holy to himself, as he has sworn to you, if you keep the commandments of the Lord your God and walk in his ways. And all the peoples of the earth shall see that you are called by the name of the Lord, and they shall be afraid of you. And the Lord will make you abound in prosperity, in the fruit of your womb and in the fruit of your livestock and in the fruit of your ground, within the land that the Lord swore to your fathers to give you. The Lord will open to you his good treasury, the heavens, to give the rain to your land in its season and to bless all the work of your hands. **And you shall lend to many nations, but you shall not borrow.** And the Lord will make you the head and not the tail, and you shall only go up and not down, if you obey the commandments of the Lord your God, which I command you today, being careful to do them, and if you do not turn aside from any of the words that I command you today, to the right hand or to the left, to go after other gods to serve them."

However, the Lord, in Deuteronomy 28, also gives us stern warnings regarding the curses for disobedience. We find in Deuteronomy 28:43-44 the following: "The sojourner who is among you shall rise higher and higher above you, and you shall come down lower and lower. **He shall lend to you, and you shall not lend to him. He shall be the head, and you shall be the tail.**" In the curses for disobedience, we also find confusion, madness, frustration, afflictions, and aliens from different lands invading their borders. America's southern border is now wide open, and there is now confusion, frustration, and affliction upon our land. Also, in 1985 and for the first time since World War I, America is a debtor nation and is now the largest in the world. China is the largest creditor nation globally and the largest holder of US Government debt.

We will now illustrate what happens to a nation when we remove God from our society, leading to spiritual bankruptcy, financial bankruptcy, and ultimately captivity to a foreign power. We begin with Madalyn Murray O'Hair (April 13, 1919 – September 29, 1995), an American Activist supporting Atheism and the separation of church and state. O'Hair was responsible for the landmark court case called *Abington School District v. Schempp* in 1963, which the Supreme Court heard. The Supreme Court ruled that officially sanctioned mandatory Bible reading in American public schools was unconstitutional. The prior year in 1962, the Supreme Court ruled in the case of *Engel v. Vitale* that sponsored prayer should be prohibited in schools. In 1963, John F. Kennedy was President, and the US National Debt stood at $307.3 billion, the US Domestic Product stood at $625.1 billion, and the Debt-to-GDP ratio was 49.17 percent. With both prayer and Bible study out of the schools, we must turn our attention to Romans 1:18-32 to gain further insight into what happens to a nation and individuals when we remove God from both our lives and our society:

"For the wrath of God is revealed from heaven against all ungodliness and unrighteousness of men, who by their unrighteousness suppress the truth. For what can be known about God is plain to them, because God has shown it to them. His invisible attributes, namely, his eternal power and divine nature, have been clearly perceived, ever since the creation of the world, in the things that have been made. So they are without excuse. For although they knew God, they did not honor him as God or give thanks to him, but they became futile in their thinking, and their foolish hearts were darkened. Claiming to be wise, they became fools, and exchanged the glory of the immortal God for images resembling mortal man and birds and animals and creeping things. Therefore "God gave them up in the lusts of their hearts to impurity, to the dishonoring of their bodies among themselves, because they exchanged the truth about God for a lie and worshiped and served the creature rather than the Creator, who is blessed forever! Amen.

"For this reason God gave them up to dishonorable passions. For their women exchanged natural relations for those that are contrary to nature; and the men likewise gave up natural relations with women and were consumed with passion for one another, men committing shameless acts with men and receiving in themselves the due penalty for their error.

"And since they did not see fit to acknowledge God, God gave them up to a debased mind to do what ought not to be done. They were filled with all manner of unrighteousness, evil, covetousness, malice. They are full of envy, murder, strife, deceit, maliciousness. They are gossips, slanderers, haters of God, insolent, haughty, boastful, inventors of evil, disobedient to parents, foolish, faithless, heartless, ruthless. Though they know God's righteous decree that those who practice such things deserve to die, they not only do them but give approval to those who practice them."

It is evident that when God's existence is denied, and His truth and moral absolutes are suppressed due to unrighteousness, the culture will begin to descend into rampant spiritual and moral decay. Once prayer, bible study, and all absolutes of truth were removed, we saw as a nation the outcome when the Supreme Court ruled on the case called *Roe v. Wade* in 1973, legalizing abortion. In 1974, Richard Nixon was President, and the US National Debt stood at $476.8 billion, the US Gross Domestic Product stood at $1.5 trillion, and the Debt-to-GDP ratio was 31.8 percent. What happened to the US National Debt since the legalization of abortion? For that answer, we turn to Barack Obama's second term in office, which ended in 2016. At this point, the US National Debt exploded to $19 trillion, the US Gross Domestic Product stood at $18.4 trillion, and the Debt-to-GDP ratio was 102.95 percent. What happened in Barack Obama's second term in office? On June 26, 2015, the Supreme Court struck down all bans on same-sex marriage, legalizing gay marriage in all fifty states. At the end of Donald Trump's term as President in 2020, the US National Debt stood at $26.6 trillion, the US Gross Domestic Product stood at $22.3 trillion, and the Debt-to-GDP ratio was 119.2 percent. Per the US Debt Clock, the projections for 2029 are beyond terrifying. Our US National Debt is estimated to be $87.5 trillion, our US Gross Domestic Product is estimated to be $26.8 trillion, and our Debt-to-GDP ratio is estimated to be 268.2 percent. As a result of its spiritual bankruptcy, America is now financially bankrupt.

In the *Theology of Work Bible Commentary*, we read the following: "We can note that when a national government becomes evil, the country's economy suffers. Psalm 81 is an example, for it begins with God's judgment against the nation of Israel. 'My people did not listen to my voice; Israel would not submit to me. So I gave them over to their stubborn hearts' (Ps. 81:11-12). Then it goes on to describe the economic consequences. 'O that my people would listen to me...I would feed you with the finest of the wheat, and with honey from the rock I would satisfy you' (Ps. 81:13, 16). Here, we see how national violations of God's covenant bring about scarcity and economic hardship. Had the people been faithful to God's ways, they would have experienced prosperity. Instead they have abandoned God's ways and find themselves going hungry (Ps. 81:10)."

America is finding itself under judgment by God by being held captive by the bondage of debt and forces such as the World Economic Forum and China. Because of its global position, China is now holding America in captivity. China is buying America's farmland and real estate. China manufactures most of our goods, including our prescription medications. China is also an Atheist Communist Regime. There is severe persecution against Christians in China, and we see a gradual, ongoing infiltration of Chinese-style communism into the United States. As a result of America's disobedience to God, we see the curses of disobedience from Deuteronomy 28 playing out before our eyes.

In addition, America's decision in 1962–63 to remove prayer and bible study from our schools created a dangerous void that needed to be filled. This void is now filled with a form of ideological captivity known as Cultural Marxism, and it saturates our school rooms and lecture halls. Cultural Marxism seeks to merge Karl Marx's theory of class struggle and the flaws in capitalism with a Freudian vision of erotic pleasure. This Luciferian Creed of Marxism and Freudian Psychoanalysis, complete with overt eroticism, became the foundation of our modern-day Critical Race

Theory. Critical Theory or Cultural Marxism is the destructive criticism of Christianity, Capitalism, Civil Authority, Family, Patriarchy, Hierarchy, Morality, Traditions, Sexual Restraint, Loyalty, Patriotism, Nationalism, Heredity, Ethnocentrism, Convention, and Conservatism. These beliefs must be destroyed and replaced with "new thinking," which ultimately annihilates society from within. Instead of a perceived Communist utopia built on unrestrained eroticism, we see the rise of both totalitarianism and depravity. The reason for this totalitarianism is that it demands uniformity of thought and behavior on all of us. Instead of Marx's idea of class struggle resulting from capitalism and economics, it has to do with the culture and all aspects of this class struggle. The complete wholesale destruction of our nation's Judeo-Christian foundation is at its core.

Because we have lost our moral compass, we are now moving into the darkness. As of this writing, we have seen the Eviction Moratorium extended after the Supreme Court ruled it was unlawful to do so. As a result of the Covid-19 pandemic, no less, this extension was by the Centers for Disease Control (CDC), who has no authority whatsoever to make these decisions. In addition, if a landlord violates this moratorium by seeking out back-rents from tenants, there is a $100,000 fine and a year in jail for non-compliance. Karl Marx and Friedrich Engels would be quite pleased by this confiscation of private rental properties, many of which are owned by the middle class. We are now turning private property into social property. Further, we are turning individualism built upon God-given resilience into classism and collectivism, where resilience is removed and replaced with totalitarian control.

We read in Nehemiah 8:9 the following: "And Nehemiah, who was the governor, and Ezra the priest and scribe, and the Levites who taught the people said to all the people, 'This day is holy to the Lord your God; do not mourn or weep.' For all the people wept as they heard the words of the Law." The Israelites wept because the Word of God had been lost in their nation. Will America find itself living in a day when they will weep at what they had lost upon hearing the Constitution? We read in Amos 8:11-12, "Behold, the days are coming," declares the Lord God, "when I will send a famine on the land—not a famine of bread, nor a thirst for water, but of hearing the words of the Lord. They shall wander from sea to sea, and from north to east they shall run to and fro, to seek the word of the Lord, but they shall not find it." Will America and the world find themselves in a modern-day dark age groping in blindness, searching with futility for the Light of the World?

"Our Constitution was made only for a moral
and religious people. It is wholly inadequate
to the government of any other."
John Adams

"If Congress can employ money indefinitely, for the general welfare,
and are the sole and supreme judges of the general welfare, they may
take the care of religion into their own hands; they may appoint
teachers in every state, county, and parish, and pay them out of the
public treasury; they may take into their own hands the education
of children, the establishing in like manner schools throughout the
union; they may assume the provision of the poor. Were the power
of Congress to be established in the latitude contended for, it would
subvert the very foundations, and transmute the very nature of the
limited government established by the people of America."
James Madison

"Our government is now taking so steady a course as to
show by what road it will pass to destruction, to wit, by
consolidation first, and then corruption. The engine of
consolidation will be the federal judiciary; the two other
branches the corrupting and corrupted instruments."
Thomas Jefferson

"The great object of my fear is the federal judiciary. That body,
like gravity, ever acting with noiseless foot and unalarming

advance, gaining ground step by step and holding what it gains, is engulfing insidiously the [state] governments into the jaws of that [federal government] which feeds them."
Thomas Jefferson

OIKONOMIA

"The rich consume little more than the poor, and in spite of their natural selfishness and rapacity... they divide with the poor the produce of all their improvements. They are led by an invisible hand to make nearly the same distribution of the necessaries of life, which would have been made, had the earth been divided into equal portions among all its inhabitants, and thus without intending it, without knowing it, advance the interest of the society, and afford means to the multiplication of the species."
Adam Smith—The Invisible Hand

"The desire to consume is a kind of lust. We long to have the world flow through us like air or food. We are thirsty and hungry for something that can only be carried inside bodies. But consumer goods merely bait this lust, they do not satisfy it. The consumer of commodities is invited to a meal without passion, a consumption that leads to neither satiation nor fire. He is a stranger seduced into feeding on the drippings of someone else's capital without the benefit of inner nourishment, and he is hungry at the end of the meal, depressed and weary as we all feel when lust has dragged us from the house and led us to nothing."
Lewis Hyde—The Gift: Imagination and the Erotic Life of Property

THE WORD "ECONOMY" comes from the Greek word *oikonomia*. It comprises Oikos, which means household, and Nomos, law, or management. Therefore, the word economy can be translated as household management. Because it focuses on the management of a household, this is where we derive the practice of stewardship. Inherent in this stewardship is how we utilize the biblical principles of money management. The notion of stewardship, although essential, focuses on a family unit and its aspects of production through livelihood and its related consumptive functions. This family unit is a microcosm of the national economy. On a much grander scale, we see the depth and meaning of Oikonomia from the standpoint of the Household of God and the totality of the Economy of God.

History has seen a separation of economics (Economy of God) from theology. From a theological perspective, as Christians, we spend time studying the attributes of God. These attributes include God's Holiness, Grace, Goodness, Patience, Omnipresence, Eternal and Unchanging Nature, Order and Peace, Truth, Justice, Omniscience, Omnipotence, Wrath and Jealousy, and Sovereignty. In these attributes, we also must see God's Economy, which encompasses all His creative work and His suffering through His Son Jesus Christ for the redemption of humanity. Therefore, God is the Great Economist.

Because of the Fall of man, we are in a state of alienation from God. This alienation produces scarcity. This scarcity, in turn, creates anxiety and fear, which leads to economic theories and systems that assuage this anxiety. Yet, these very theories and systems are designed from the very scarcity created from man's alienation from God. Because these economic theories and systems cater to man's sinful human nature, they become idols creating an illusion of freedom that masks the harsh reality of domination and slavery by the unregenerated elite over the masses. Jean-Jacques Rousseau said, "Man was born free, and he is everywhere in chains." These chains are created by separating God from our economic theories and systems, letting market forces abound and all too often to the detriment of the market themselves. Even Adam Smith's *Invisible Hand* was that of market forces that bring these markets into equilibrium. Some have speculated that this Invisible Hand was a reference to God; however, these market forces relied on the Newtonian concept of natural laws potentially removed from God. The Economy of God seeks to break these chains to eliminate market forces that lead to domination, slavery, and tyrannical despotism.

Even the Triune Persons of the Godhead, the Father, the Son, and the Holy Spirit, comprise what has been called the Economic Trinity. The Economic Trinity concerns the idea that each member of the Trinity carries out a specific role in the plan and outworking of human redemption. This Trinity seeks a distribution of righteousness and redemption for humanity in a communitarian fashion whereby each householder of God utilizes not just stewardship but acts as economic agents for the advancement of the Gospel for that redemption. This Trinity has found itself warring against the trinity of man's self-serving interests, creating an economic trinity of supply-demand and price. This trinity promotes fierce competition in a winner-take-all fashion because implicit in scarcity is the hidden deception that there is not enough to go around. In turn, this hidden deception promotes the amassing of wealth for the sake of its security, which is but a mere illusion. Because of man's alienation from God, it removes eternity from his eyes.

The world is seen in finite terms. The absolute magnitude of scarcity is one of time and life itself. This leads to the only constant in life, insatiable accumulation, and consumption because of the fear of death. God's Economy of Grace, Righteousness, and Redemption through the Lord Jesus Christ not only destroyed death, but He also liberated us from scarcity that will ultimately be true after the Kingdom of God has been fully established at the end of this present world order. This gives us an eternal perspective as God's fellow economic agents and stewards of His creation. Ecclesiastes 3:11 says, "He has made everything beautiful in its time. Also, he has put eternity into man's heart, yet so that he cannot find out what God has done from the beginning to the end." The Household of God demonstrates redemption and freedom whereby the household of man is one of domination and slavery. We read in Philippians 2:6-7 that Jesus "who, though he was in the form of God, did not count equality with God a thing to be grasped but emptied himself, by taking the form of a servant, being born in the likeness of men." Although most translations use the word servant, the Greek word *doulos* means slave. The Great Economist came to earth as a household slave to free this household from fear and scarcity to live a life more abundantly in Him. Jesus, as the Incarnation of God and Great Economist, distributed to His believers the righteousness of God, demonstrating He is the sustainer of all creation and giving us the knowledge that there is more than enough through His presence to go around. In 2 Corinthians 8:9, Paul informs the Corinthian Church, "For you know the grace of our Lord Jesus Christ, that though he was rich, yet for your sake, he became poor so that you by his poverty might become rich." Paul reveals the mystery of the Economy of God. God, the Great Economist through Jesus Christ, left the opulence of heaven which no eye has seen in one of the most significant exchanges the world has ever known. He laid aside His riches and took up the impoverishment of this world unto Himself to give us the wealth of a peace that passes all understanding. He assuaged our hearts and minds to know that all our needs would be met not through accumulation and consumption but through the Spirit of God, who gives all things to those who believe in Him. Jesus Christ, through our redemption in Him, is building the Household of God. We are His Oikos, His Household.

In numerous chapters of this book, we have seen the households of men such as Karl Marx, John Maynard Keynes, Thomas Piketty, and Klaus Schwab who have sought to use economics as a way of domination and control over others. We can see how Socialism and Communism are in constant opposition against the Household of God and His Economy. These economic theories and systems, especially Communism by its very design, prey on this scarcity because Communism distorts all aspects of production, leading to shortages of food and goods, causing a never-ending cycle of destruction until it leads to its failure. Is it any wonder why Communists seek to remove God and Christianity from society? In suppressing the revelation of God through His Word and in the world He created, they attempt to eliminate God (Romans 1:18-21). The Great Economist, whose very nature and being is that of abundance and creative power assures us that our faith and trust in Him will sustain all of our needs. As hard as a man may try, it is God Himself who sustains the entirety of His creation. John Maynard Keynes, toward the end of his life in 1946, said to Henry Clay, a professor of social economics and advisor to the Bank of England, "I find myself more and more relying on a solution to our problem on the invisible hand which I tried to eject from economic thinking twenty years ago." The Philosopher King and Self Appointed Monetary Alchemist lamented the outcome of his interventions beseeching the invisible hand to his rescue. Perhaps Keynes had finally given up his war not against the invisible hand but of God. He was now facing his exhausted, finite nature. He was now facing God Himself on the precipice of death. All of us must ask ourselves regarding our households and financial lives, are we fighting at times against the Great Economist? Do we see ourselves as part of the Household of God, or are we acting independently of it swayed by the culture of accumulation and consumption? Do we fully live with the understanding that we are the living stones of the Temple and the responsibility it means for our lives? Solomon, who was considered the wealthiest man in the world, said in Ecclesiastes 1:14, "I have seen everything that is done under the sun, and behold, all is vanity and a striving after wind." No matter what contrived economic systems man produces, they will always lead to idolatry, domination, and subjugation. Because they are removed from God they are all striving after the wind.

"Therefore I tell you, do not be anxious about your life, what you will eat or what you will drink, nor about your body, what you will put on. Is not life more than food, and the body more than clothing? Look at the birds of the air: they neither sow nor reap nor gather into barns, and yet your heavenly Father feeds them. Are you not of more value than they? And which of you by being anxious can add a single hour to his span of life? And why are you anxious about clothing? Consider the lilies of the field, how they grow: they neither toil nor spin, yet I tell you, even Solomon in all his glory was not arrayed like one of these. But if God so clothes the grass of the field, which today is alive and tomorrow is thrown into the oven, will he not much more clothe you, O you of little faith? Therefore do not be anxious, saying, 'What shall

we eat?' or 'What shall we drink?' or 'What shall we wear?' For the Gentiles seek after all these things, and your heavenly Father knows that you need them all. But seek first the kingdom of God and his righteousness, and all these things will be added to you.

Jesus Christ—Matthew 6:25-33

COME OUT OF HER MY PEOPLE

*"Then I heard another voice from heaven saying, 'Come out of her, my
people, lest you take part in her sins, lest you share in her plagues'"*
Revelation 18:4

IN OUR LAST chapter, we discussed the importance of the Economy of
God. We can also see that God, through Jesus Christ, is also building
His Household. In addition, the Greek word *oikos* (house, household)
can also mean the House of God, the tabernacle, and the family of God.
In addition, *oikodome* implies the act of building up, edification and
buildings. In 1 Corinthians 3:9-11 (NRSV), Paul writes the following to
the Corinthian Church: "According to the grace of God given to me, like
a skilled master builder I laid a foundation, and someone else is building
on it. Each builder must choose with care how to build on it. For no
one can lay any foundation other than the one that has been laid; that
foundation is Jesus Christ."

Further in 1 Corinthians 3:16-17 (NRSV), Paul writes, "Do you not
know that you are God's temple and that God's Spirit dwells in you? If
anyone destroys God's temple, God will destroy that person. For God's
temple is holy, and you are that temple." Lastly, Paul writes in 2 Corinthians 6:16 (NRSV), "What agreement has the temple of God with idols?
For we are the temple of the living God; as God said, 'I will live in them
and walk among them, and I will be their God, and they shall be my
people.'" Also, in 1 Peter 2:4-5 (NRSV), we read the following: "Come to
him, a living stone, though rejected by mortals yet chosen and precious
in God's sight, and like living stones, let yourselves be built into a spiritual

house, to be a holy priesthood, to offer spiritual sacrifices acceptable to God through Jesus Christ."

There is great importance to these scriptures as it pertains to our stewardship. As Christians, we are to adhere to the biblical principles of money and stewardship, for the implications of our stewardship reveal that as believers, we are the living stones of the temple. As such, we are also part of the Household of God. We are all part of an economic tapestry meticulously woven together by God, the Great Economist, as householders stewarding the Living Temple of God and His Kingdom. The urgency of this cannot be underestimated because we are standing in the gap between two economic systems. The first is predatory capitalism through its lending function, leading to the bondage of debt. This form of capitalism appeals to the hedonic nature of consumerism. We read in 1 John 2:16, "For all that is in the world—the desires of the flesh and the desires of the eyes and pride of life—is not from the Father but is from the world." In more modern terms, this is sensualism, materialism, and egotism. This predatory capitalism works with various forms of social media platforms to provoke covetousness in ourselves and others. Essentially, this leads to the marketing of materialistic pursuits based on that covetousness which creates a scarcity in our hearts and minds of not having enough to keep up with the Joneses. Its design foisters perceived needs versus real needs, which become consumption for the sake of consumption facilitated by debt. Affluence or, more accurately, Affluenza can also lead to pride. In his book *Money, Possessions and Eternity*, Randy Alcorn writes, "One uglier manifestation of pride is elitism, an illusion of superiority over others that's held by a privileged class. Elitism is at the heart of racism, nationalism, and denominationalism. It is sometimes the driving force behind private clubs, restaurants, hotels, schools, fraternities, sororities, certain churches, and countless affiliations." Further, he writes, "The well-to-do Pharisees lived and breathed a prosperity theology, labeling everyone beneath their social caste as 'sinners.'

At the other end of the spectrum are socialism and communism, which are nothing more than atheistic materialism. In this, we see the attempt to usurp predatory capitalism run amok, which has created the condition of the haves and the have nots ushering in demands for equality. This then leads to communism, whereby the government is now in control, removing economic freedom by oppressive measures. In some cases, we see the merger of government and corporations, which creates a far worsening chasm between rich and poor instead of alleviating inequality. These systems can and do go to extremes. However, when it does not turn predatory, capitalism is undoubtedly a better alternative than communism. No matter what economic system we are dealing with, sin and man's alienation from God are what distorts them all. Further, Satan is the lord of materialism, his siren song of never enough beckons many souls into a trance setting a grievous trap with eternal consequences.

The Household of God stands between the gap of these two economic extremes. As believers in Christ and members of the Household of God, we are sanctified, meaning we are separate and apart from these prevailing economic systems. As Christians, we are told to be in the world but not of the world. Since we are in the world as believers, we utilize the necessary financial products for savings and future retirement. However, we must be mindful not to be lured into the culture around us. We now turn to the Parable of the Ten Minas found in Luke 19:11-27, which says the following: "As they heard these things, he proceeded to tell a parable, because he was near to Jerusalem, and because they supposed that the kingdom of God was to appear immediately. He said therefore, "A nobleman went into a far country to receive for himself a kingdom and then return. Calling ten of his servants, he gave them ten minas, and said to them, '**Engage in business until I come**.' But his citizens hated him and sent a delegation after him, saying, 'We do not want this man to reign over us.' When he returned, having received the kingdom, he ordered these servants to whom he had given the money to be called to him, that he might know what they had gained by doing business. The first came before him, saying, 'Lord, your mina has made ten minas more.' And he said to him, 'Well done, good servant! Because you have been faithful in a very little, you shall have authority over ten cities.' And the second came, saying, 'Lord, your mina has made five minas.' And he said to him, 'And you are to be over five cities.' Then another came, saying, 'Lord, here is your mina, which I kept laid away in a handkerchief; for I was afraid of you, because you are a severe man. You take what you did not deposit, and reap what you did not sow.' He said to him, 'I will condemn you with your own words, you wicked servant! You knew that I was a severe man, taking what I did not deposit and reaping what I did not sow? Why then did you not put my money in the bank, and at my coming I might have collected it with interest?' And he said to those who stood by, 'Take the mina from him, and give it to the one who has the ten minas.' And they said to him, 'Lord, he has ten minas!' 'I tell you that to everyone who has, more will be given, but from the one who has not, even what he has will be taken away. But as for these enemies of mine, who did not want me to reign over them, bring them here and slaughter them before me.'"

The Parable of the Minas also has its counterpart in Matthew called the Parable of the Talents. These Minas and Talents are the capital the Lord Jesus and Great Economist invests in His believers. This capital represents our natural talents, abilities, interests, personality, financial means, and spiritual gifts, which have been endowed to us by the creator. Jesus is giving us resources to perpetuate the Economy and Kingdom of God. In the *Theology of Work Bible Commentary*, it says the following: "This parable makes explicit that citizens of God's Kingdom are responsible to work toward God's goals and purposes. In this parable, the king tells his servants directly what he expects them to do, namely, to invest his money. This specific calling or command makes it clear that preaching, healing, and evangelism (the apostles' callings) are not the only things God calls people to do. Of course, not everyone in God's Kingdom is called to be an investor, either. In this parable, only three of the country's residents are called to be investors. The point is that acknowledging Jesus as King requires working toward his purposes in whatever field of work you do."

The Greek word *pragmateuomai*, depending on the biblical translation, means to put this money to work, do business, buy and sell, trade, and lastly, in the King James Version, it says, "occupy till I come." The word "occupy" can be seen as a foreign power occupying another nation the way we saw Rome occupying Jerusalem. Dear Reader, we are purposefully set apart as occupiers for both the Economy of God and the Kingdom of God. We are the occupiers from the Lord Jesus Christ's Spiritual Kingdom, and He is giving us provisions to maintain our occupation of this foreign territory. We are to hold our ground and stand in this gap because this is a spiritual battle between the Household of God and the Household of Man. From a purely economic standpoint, we, through Christ, work to take these competing economic systems of predatory capitalism and communism and bring them to the biblical principles of the Economy of God. As occupiers, we do not take on the culture we are occupying. Therefore, we must guard our hearts, humble ourselves and focus our minds on the Word of God, practice His ways and yield only to Him. We must heed the words of Ephesians 5:15-16, which says, "Look carefully then how you walk, not as unwise but as wise, making the best use of the time because the days are evil." Where we stand is Holy ground, and each step we take are those of an occupying ambassador in a foreign land sharing through our livelihood and stewardship the Economy of God and His Kingdom.

As the living stones of the Temple and as members in the Household of God, we must turn to scripture, letting it read our hearts and our minds. In the chapter on the Financial Crisis of 33 AD, we saw how Jesus entered the Temple and overturned the money changers' tables and proclaimed that His House shall be called a house of prayer. The physical Temple in Jerusalem was in a state of financial corruption. In prayer, we must ask ourselves, and the Lord, is there a money changer in our hearts, and do our lives reflect a house of prayer? It is imperative to understand that our personal stewardship reflects our hearts. Therefore, we must ask ourselves and the Lord if certain things in our lives are idols we exchange in worship for the one true Living God. We must at all times seek the Lord in prayer and allow the Holy Spirit to purify our hearts and minds asking him to remove these idols, for we occupy a battlefield filled with temptations. This is a battlefield with many snares that can entrap us to the cares of this world. The lust of the eyes, the lust of the flesh, and the pride for life are the trinity of this world that has held many a believer in captivity to it. On the lust of the eyes, William Gurnall, in his book *The Christian in Complete Armour*, writes the following: "The apostle refers here to those temptations drawn from the world's treasury. And it is the eye which first commits adultery with them. As the unclean eye looks upon another man's wife, so the covetous eye looks on another's wealth to lust after it. Consider what tragic effects this temptation has on Ahab when he covets Naboth's vineyard. To gain only a few acres which do not add much to a king's revenues, he swims to it in the owner's blood. Only faith can permanently blind lusting eyes and give clear insight into the sufficiency of God's grace. Satan lures the soul to venture out into lying and taking the wedge of gold like a carrot dangled before a donkey; but faith simply convinces the soul of God's fatherly care. This faith teaches the soul to counter, 'I am well provided for already, Satan; I do not need your donation; why should I play the thief for something which God has promised to give me? Let your conversation be without covetousness; and be content with such things as ye have: for he hath said, I will never leave thee, nor forsake thee (Heb 13:5). How can you possibly lack anything when God's promise commands His riches? Let him who is without God in the world struggle to survive in Satan's worthless will; but Christian, you are free to live on the inheritance of your faith."

Brothers and sisters in Christ, we have a glorious inheritance which is the sustenance of our faith. Our livelihoods and work equip us with an income not only for our gain and personal savings but also for the Economy of God and His Kingdom. Because of this inheritance, we have been given the biblical principles of money management and stewardship, which we follow in faith. As Christians, we cannot be impacted by the materialistic world system and, in doing so, idolize wealth. Nor should we overly identify with the poor only to romanticize poverty. Puritan William Ames wrote, "Riches are morally neither good nor bad, but things indifferent which men may use either well or ill." Puritan John Downame wrote that "The mean (median) estate is much to be preferred before the greatest prosperity. The mean estate preserveth us from the forgetfulness of God, irreligion, and profaneness." These quotes reinforce the Puritan idea of moderation. The hallmark of that moderation is contentment and trust in God's ability to provide. In Philippians 4:10-13, Paul says, "I rejoiced in the Lord greatly that now at length you have revived your concern for me. You were indeed concerned for me, but you had no opportunity. Not that I am speaking of being in need, for I have learned in whatever situation I am to be content. I know how to be brought low, and I know how to abound. In any and every circumstance, I have learned the secret of facing plenty and hunger, abundance and need. I can do all things through him who strengthens me."

The world's economic systems are spiritual battlefields working against the Household of God. We see in Marxism the desire to remove private property, install heavy progressive tax systems and abolish inheritances. This desire is to usurp the Throne of God and take control of God's possessions. The abolishment of inheritances should come as no surprise since we have been given an inheritance representing the Kingdom of God as believers. We see in John Maynard Keynes a man who had a loathing for the Puritans and their inclination toward thrift and godly enterprise through biblical morality, stewardship, and a strong work ethic. Therefore, it should not be a shock that John Maynard Keynes would coin the phrase the Euthanasia of the Rentier, which means the painless or mercy killing of the middle class through interest rate manipulation. We now see a direct attack against the Householder of God and why John Maynard Keynes sought to euthanize them financially. This euthanasia is nothing less than an attempt to siphon away the resources of God for His Economy and Kingdom. However, by far the most debilitating condition for the Householders of God is the use of debt. Debt redirects the resources God invested in us for His Economy and Kingdom purposes for self-serving, self-indulgent pursuits. It forces the Christian to be focused on the cares of the world, desecrating the Household of God. By its very nature, debt implies that we cannot rely on the Lord, and therefore we take matters into our hands by denying Him the opportunity to provide. Dependence on predatory capitalism is Satan's most significant achievement against the Household of God. As occupiers in a foreign land, we reduce our ability to stand in the gap because our "provisions" have been squandered, allowing the enemy to further their march against the Economy and Kingdom of God.

In Revelation 18:1-4, we are introduced to the Fall of Babylon, "After this I saw another angel coming down from heaven, having great authority, and the earth was made bright with his glory. And he called out with a mighty voice, 'Fallen, fallen is Babylon the great! She has become a dwelling place for demons, a haunt for every unclean spirit, a haunt for every unclean bird, a haunt for every unclean and detestable beast. For all nations have drunk the wine of the passion of her sexual immorality, and the kings of the earth have committed immorality with her, and the merchants of the earth have grown rich from the power of her luxurious living.' Then I heard another voice from heaven saying, 'Come out of her, my people, lest you take part in her sins, lest you share in her plagues.'" *The Theology of Work Bible Commentary* says, "The lesson that God would judge a city for its economic practices is a sobering thought. Economics is clearly a moral issue in the book of Revelation. The fact that much of the condemnation appears to stem from its self-indulgence should hit with particular force at modern consumer culture, where the constant search for more and better can lead to a myopic focus on satisfying real or imagined material needs. But the most worrisome thing of all is that Babylon looks so close to the New Jerusalem. God did create a good world; we are meant to enjoy life; God does delight in the beautiful things of earth. If the world system were a self-evident cesspool, the temptation for Christians to fall to its allures would be small. It is precisely the genuine benefits of technological advances and extensive trading networks that constitute the danger. Babylon promises all the glories of Eden, without the intrusive presence of God. It slowly but inexorably twists the good gifts of God—economic interchange, agricultural abundance, diligent craftsmanship into the service of false gods." Fellow Christians, the only way to come out of Babylon is to know about these economic systems warring against us as we stand in the gap between them. We must hold steadfast to the truth that Jesus Christ has overcome the world, and we must occupy till He comes!

> *"I am coming soon. Hold fast what you have, so that no one may seize your crown. The one who conquers, I will make him a pillar in the temple of my God. Never shall he go out of it, and I will write on him the name of my God, and the name of the city of my God, the new Jerusalem, which comes down from my God out of heaven, and my own new name."*
>
> Revelation 3:11-12

> *"Then I saw a new heaven and a new earth, for the first heaven and the first earth had passed away, and the sea was no more. And I saw the holy city, new Jerusalem, coming down out of heaven from God, prepared as a bride adorned for her husband. And I heard a loud voice from the throne saying, 'Behold, the dwelling place of God is with man. He will dwell with them, and they will be his people, and God himself will be with them as their God. He will wipe away every tear from their eyes, and death shall be no more, neither shall there be mourning, nor crying, nor pain anymore, for the former things have passed away.'"*
>
> Revelation 21:1-4

SURRENDER

"Now the serpent was more crafty than any other beast of the field that the Lord God had made. He said to the woman, 'Did God actually say, "You shall not eat of any tree in the garden?"' And the woman said to the serpent, 'We may eat of the fruit of the trees in the garden, but God said, "You shall not eat of the fruit of the tree that is in the midst of the garden, neither shall you touch it, lest you die."' But the serpent said to the woman, 'You will not surely die. For God knows that when you eat of it your eyes will be opened, and you will be like God, knowing good and evil."

Genesis 3:1-5

"The devil's finest trick is to persuade you that he does not exist."

Charles Baudelaire—Poet

W E END WITH the beginning when God granted dominion of the earth to man. He commanded that Adam would be the one who would rule and subdue all the earth. He would be an earthly king ruling and reigning under the Sovereign Authority of the Lord God who granted this dominion of the earth but never gave up His Sovereignty for Adam and Eve or any of its beneficiaries. God instituted the perfect economy for which this created couple would thrive. The one who masquerades as an Angel of Light appeared in that perfect world and led Adam and Eve to their fall through deception. In Genesis 3:18-19, in addition to the curse of death, Adam's Crown of Perfection would be exchanged for a crown of thorns, thistles, and hardship as he would now labor by the sweat of his brow. The magnificent perfection of God's

Economic System was now fractured by deceit, deception, and false promises. The Household of God was now compromised until another King could be found to rule and reign and bring this Household to its final redemption.

God knew before the foundation of the world this fate that would befall humanity. In a remarkable reversal, He sent our Lord and Savior Jesus Christ and Great Economist. Jesus would take upon His Head the Crown of Thorns to restore the Household of God, unleashing upon the world the Dominion of the True King of Kings and Lord of Lords. No longer would we labor in the thorns and thistles by hardship and the sweat of our brows. Our work and our labor would be turned into their proper function. The Hebrew word *avodah* is the same for work and worship. We read in Colossians 3:23-24; "Whatever you do, work heartily, as for the Lord and not for men, knowing that from the Lord you will receive the inheritance as your reward. You are serving the Lord Christ." Our labors are no longer in vain but are for the Lord Jesus Christ in all that we do because when the Great Economist wore the Crown of Thorns, He let us know that in Him, nothing is secular in this world. For in Him, there is unity and wholeness, which is in harmony with God's Design. The conflict we see all around us began with man's rebellion against God in the Garden of Eden when they ate of the fruit of the tree of the knowledge of Good and Evil. A perverted dualism has twisted our hearts where we separate the secular and the sacred. This dualism has caused many Christians to abdicate their stewardship responsibilities over many areas of life, including the realm of economics.

The realm of economics puts us in peril because it is from this place that comes all the world's temptations. For money does enchant the desires of our lusts, fueled by the greed of our hearts whose longings are never satisfied absent the Lord. This vacant heart that cries out in the wilderness of the world is longing for a savior. The deceiver knows the siren song of seduction well, and he works against the Household of God to reduce our effectiveness in this world. For hidden in the world of economics is the battle of dependence. Who do we depend on? Do we depend on the false god of government to rescue us from our self-created sin-filled conditions? Do we depend on Wall Street to give us riches and abundance that have led many astray in the thorns and thistles of worldly cares and concerns? Do we depend on our financial portfolios, businesses, and achievements which are nothing more than reliance on deaf, dumb, lifeless, unforgiving idols that lead to delusional vain imaginings of who we think God is?

Many are horrified at the financial condition of this nation and the world. Through our incessant greed and unquenched desires, we have built an economic system of debt with no real substance. The world now has seen its materialism fueled by reckless consumption eat away at the foundations of sound economics. Here we now stand between the two economic extremes of predatory capitalism through its lending function and those demanding a Great Reset of the world which is nothing but the false gospel of utopianism. Ephesians 6:16-18 says, "In all circumstances take up the shield of faith, with which you can extinguish all the flaming darts of the evil one; and take the helmet of salvation, and the sword of the Spirit, which is the word of God, praying at all times in the Spirit, with all prayer and supplication." The Ruler of this World uses economics as one of his flaming darts. He snares the soul with the false promises of a life rich and abundant apart from Jesus Christ. He lures us with the same temptations as he did in the Garden of Eden if we only bow down and worship him. He assuages our spiritual hunger by enticing economists to turn stones into bread to feed the masses of those whose souls are tossed about like lost ships in a furious tempest. He offers baubles, jewels, gold, and silver with promises of fame and fortune. He draws our attention to bright shiny objects that capture the lust of our eyes with no benefit in the end. Our hearts become more shallow as we seek comfort and peace in a world of such uncertainty.

Now the world was imprisoned by a virus. Entire economies were shut down, and we do not know the long-term implications of these measures. Yet, we are being told if we bow down and worship our governments and do as we are told, we will be given all the freedom in the world. Behind the scenes, organizations like the World Economic Forum seek to reimagine the world in their own image. They are the self-appointed kings with their fleshly crowns pretending to be gods. What we are witnessing is no longer a flaming dart. The Adversary, the Devil, has now released the flaming arrow of utopianism that is encircling the world. Its embers are falling to earth, setting it aflame. We are witnessing the rise of Global Authoritarianism, which has never been seen in world history. What Satan cannot do by force, he shall do by subtle treachery, fear, and fraud.

Christians, we must stand firm in this gap and remember the words of David from Psalm 57:4, "My soul is among lions; I lie among the sons of men, Who are set on fire, Whose teeth are spears and arrows, And their tongue a sharp sword." We must not be lulled to sleep by our complacency and comforts or the Luciferian Lullaby of Communist Utopianism whose ruler is none other than Satan. We must stay vigilant in our faith and remember we are spiritual sojourners occupying a foreign territory. One cannot help but think of the memoir, *This Saved Us*, by Silvester Krcmery. He was a political prisoner in totalitarian Czechoslovakia who wrote, "Material things which mankind regarded as certainties were fleeting and illusory, while faith, which the world considered to be ephemeral, was the most reliable and the most powerful of foundations. The more I depended on faith, the stronger I became." It was Jesus Christ who said in Matthew 6:19-21, "Do not lay up for yourselves treasures on earth, where moth and rust destroy and where thieves break in and steal, but lay up for yourselves treasures in heaven, where neither moth nor rust destroys and where thieves do not break in and steal. For where your treasure is, there your heart will be also" During times of trials and tribulations, it is our faith in Jesus that is our only foundation. No matter what the circumstances may be, God is Sovereign over it all and will take these circumstances, whether times of prosperity and freedom, depressions, recessions, Covid-19 complete with lockdowns and tyranny, and bring them to His plans and His purposes. In the end, it is all so we can know Jesus Christ and bring glory and honor to Him. Satan seeks to divide and conquer the Household of God, knowing that a house divided against itself cannot stand. However, a house united in the faith of Christ will stand victorious not by its own doing but by the One who conquered Satan on the cross once and for all.

We must remember the words of Jeremiah 17:9, which says, "The heart is deceitful above all things." We cannot depend on anything except the Lord Jesus Christ. Our life is a paradox, for with our rebellion against God comes a servitude to others that leads to tyranny. Only our submission and surrender to the Will of God leads to true freedom. Jesus Christ emptied Himself in complete surrender to become a Household Slave to liberate the Household of God. The King of Kings and Lord of Lords wearing the blood-soaked Crown of Thorns gave us true freedom in Him because He is our Jubilee releasing us from our bondage to this world. Jesus Christ is the one who said, in Matthew 11:28-30, "Come to me, all who labor and are heavy laden, and I will give you rest. Take my yoke upon you, and learn from me, for I am gentle and lowly in heart, and you will find rest for your souls. For my yoke is easy, and my burden is light." When we finally surrender ourselves to the Lord Jesus Christ, He and He alone breaks the chains of our captivity. He puts His arm around us, comforting us with His Word, and allows the Holy Spirit to lift the veil from our eyes, healing our blindness so we can finally see the Great Economic Deception. Dear reader, in the end, it has all been a battle for our hearts, minds, and souls to tempt and lure us away from the Lord Jesus Christ who said, "I am the Way, the Truth, and the Life."

"And you shall know the truth, and the truth will set you free."
Jesus Christ—John 8:32

"Understanding is the reward of faith. Therefore,
seek not to understand that you may believe,
but believe that you may understand."
Augustine—Tractate on the Gospel of John

O sacred Head surrounded
By crown of piercing thorn!
O bleeding Head, so wounded,
Reviled and put to scorn!
The pow'r of death comes o'er you,
The glow of life decays,
Yet angel hosts adore you
And tremble as they gaze.
I see your strength and vigor
All fading in the strife,
And death with cruel rigor,
Bereaving you of life;
O agony and dying!
O love to sinners free!
Jesus, all grace supplying,
O turn your face on me.
In this, your bitter passion,
Good Shepherd, think of me
With your most sweet compassion,
Unworthy though I be:
Beneath your cross abiding
Forever would I rest,
In your dear love confiding,
And with your presence blest.

Bernard of Clairvaux

ABOUT THE AUTHOR

Theresa J. Yarosh, CFP®, CLU®, ChFC®, CKA

I HAVE SPENT over twenty years in the financial services industry, specializing in the impact of healthcare costs in retirement. I steward two companies, Macro Wealth Management, LLC, and Main Street Medigap, LLC. These two companies work in tandem to project healthcare costs in retirement plans. At the onset of the pandemic, I saw an alarming situation unfolding not only in the United States but globally. Throughout my twenties and early thirties, I found myself reading books by Murray Rothbard, Ludwig von Mises, F.A. Hayek, and Henry Hazlitt. These economists were always upholding a free-market society based on private property rights. Also, I was fascinated by books on the depression of the 1930s, which led me to the writings of Irving Fisher. For me, the most eye-opening book was *The Creature from Jekyll Island* by G. Edward Griffin. This book is a profound exposé on our Central Banking system, instituted by the Federal Reserve Act of 1913 under President Woodrow Wilson. He was the catalyst for launching the progressive era, which has led to severe economic implications for our nation. During all these years of reading and research, I felt that I was being prepared for something in my life, but I did not know what it was. On November 17, 2012, I gave my life to Christ and began studying the Bible and books on Jesus Christ and Christianity.

Before the pandemic began, I enrolled in the Certified Kingdom Advisor program and was certified in December 2020. The Certified Kingdom Advisor® is a designation granted by Kingdom Advisors to individuals who have demonstrated themselves to be believers in Jesus

Christ, apply biblical wisdom in counsel, incorporate biblical principles in their financial advice, are technically competent, and practice biblical stewardship in their personal and professional life. When I was studying to become a Certified Kingdom Advisor, I also began writing in April 2020. All of that reading and research so many years earlier in my life allowed me to see the direction we are now, as a nation and as a global society, moving in. As my writing unfolded, I realized that this was the very moment I was being prepared for, and it was to write this book and do so from a biblical worldview. It is a book that demonstrates how the Lord lifted the veil from my own eyes to see this Great Economic Deception. I know that this book was written on my heart before the foundation of the world. In so many ways, this book is the song of my soul and for a time such as this.

CPSIA information can be obtained
at www.ICGtesting.com
Printed in the USA
JSHW022122040522
25590JS00003B/18